One Black Man's Journey From
Ivy League to Prision and Back Again

BECOMING *Ken*

KEN MILLER

EDITED BY STEFAN JUNAEUS

THOUGHT
LEADERS
PRESS

Published By Thought Leaders Press

Produced by Signature Message LLC

Foreword Written By Tim Storey

Edited By Stefan Junaeus

E-Book ISBN: 978-1-966170-11-2

Softcover ISBN: 978-1-966170-00-6

Hardcover ISBN: 978-1-966170-12-9

THOUGHT
LEADERS
PRESS

CONTENTS

LETTER FROM THE EDITOR
STEFAN JUNAEUS

EDITOR & CHIEF OF THOUGHT LEADERS PRESS

Every book I have the privilege to work on holds a unique place in my heart, but some resonate on a deeper frequency —a frequency of profound transformation, raw authenticity, and relentless courage. Ken Miller's journey is exactly that kind of story.

As Editor-in-Chief of Thought Leaders Press, I often find myself guiding authors through the delicate art of turning personal pain into purposeful narrative. With Ken, however, I quickly realized my role was more witness than guide. His words needed no prompting; they flowed naturally from a heart genuinely dedicated to healing—not just his own, but yours and mine, too.

Ken's story embodies what I believe to be the essence of real breakthrough: facing the uncomfortable truths, embracing radical honesty, and taking ownership of every chapter—especially the darkest ones. Ken shows us that redemption is not a distant, unattainable ideal but a tangible reality, accessible to anyone willing to embrace grace, forgive the person in the mirror, and courageously rewrite their narrative.

In my book, "Your Breakthrough Year," I write about transformation as a journey of intentional choice and disciplined action. Ken's life powerfully exemplifies these principles in action, providing a masterclass in resilience and renewal. As you read his story, you'll discover the quiet strength that emerges from vulnerability, the empowerment found in accountability, and the profound freedom born from extending grace to oneself.

My sincere hope is that Ken's journey becomes a catalyst for your own. Whether you're standing at a crossroads, looking for clarity, or seeking courage to open those "unfinished doors," I invite you to lean into Ken's story. Let his truth illuminate your path and empower your next step forward.

Here's to your breakthrough,

Stefan Andreas Junaeus
Editor-in-Chief, Thought Leaders Press

FOREWORD
TIM STOREY

Life often takes us places we never intended to go. It breaks us down, challenges our beliefs, and tests the very limits of our endurance. But what truly defines us is not how far we fall, but how courageously we rise. Every setback is a setup for a comeback—and no story proves that truth more powerfully than the one you're about to experience.

Ken Miller's journey is raw, authentic, and profoundly inspiring. From the darkest streets and deepest despair, Ken found himself trapped in a cycle that many never escape. Addiction, homelessness, incarceration—these were not just stops along his journey; they were battlefields where he fought for his soul. But through each trial, Ken discovered something vital: resilience isn't about avoiding failure, it's about rising after you've been knocked down, again and again.

In my work as America's Comeback Coach, I've witnessed countless transformations. I've seen people rise from financial ruin, emotional devastation, and spiritual emptiness. Yet, even with all the comebacks I've championed, Ken's story stands uniquely powerful. It's a testament not only to his determination but to the power of grace—grace extended by others, and perhaps most importantly, grace he learned to offer himself.

Within these pages, you will encounter honesty so profound it might make you uncomfortable, truths so sharp they could pierce your heart, and redemption so beautiful it will move your soul. Ken's story doesn't gloss over his mistakes; instead, he courageously confronts them, sharing every scar as proof of survival and every lesson as fuel for change. He demonstrates that our past never has to predict our future—that we can always write a new chapter, no matter how many previous ones have ended badly.

As you read, I encourage you to reflect on your own journey. Where have you stumbled? Where might you still be holding onto secrets, fears, or regrets? Ken reminds us all that each new day is an opportunity, each setback an invitation to rise higher. His life, now filled with mentorship, purpose, and compassion, is proof that transformation is not only possible —it's within your reach.

So lean into Ken's story, absorb his wisdom, and let it inspire you. Because in life, as Ken so powerfully illustrates, it's never too late to become who you were meant to be.

Your Comeback is Now,
Tim Storey

INTRODUCTION

Catalyst: ˈka-tə-ləst (n.) — *an agent that provokes or speeds significant change or action*

Cockroaches scurried the instant the door opened, their glossy backs scattering across grimy tiles. I jolted awake, my heart ramming against my ribcage, and for a moment, I couldn't remember where I was. Then I realized: a utility closet in a rundown Reno rooming house, stinking of mildew and ammonia, was the closest thing I had to a home.

My company these last three days had been brooms, mops, a bucket of stale water, and a legion of insects no landlord wanted. We had that in common—both they and I were unwelcome. And now, hovering over me with an angry glare, was the middle-aged Black man who owned the building. Or at least he had enough authority to kick me out.

"Get up," he barked. "I'm callin' the cops if you're still here in five minutes."

Call the Cops...

The threat echoed. The truth was, one phone call from him—five minutes—and I'd be back in a police wagon. My heart hammered. I started gathering my few pathetic belongings: a busted lighter, a half-empty can of warm Natural Ice beer, and a broken glass pipe. These were the essentials I carried, day in, day out, like a soldier's kit.

As I walked outside, the September sun of Reno felt too bright. I'd been holed up in that closet, avoiding the cruelty of the streets while descending deeper into that special brand of self-pity that devours all dignity. A line from Chaka Khan's "Through the Fire" drifted through my mind. I'd been hearing it everywhere lately, that or Kanye West's remix, "Through the Wire." Every time, it reminded me of how my own jaw had been broken—not once but twice—and how I'd ended up with my mouth wired shut, forced to survive through unimaginable pain.

How did I, an Ivy League graduate from Dartmouth, become a crack-addicted drifter sleeping in a closet?

I could blame all sorts of things: a childhood overshadowed by my father's anger, repeated letdowns, the spinning lure of quick highs, the trauma, the street hustles, my own insecurities that ran deeper than any mold in that dingy closet. But the simplest explanation is that I made a thousand and one bad choices, each fueling the next.

The Cracked Road to the Broom Closet

Before I try to offer any insights, let me rewind to just weeks before that landlord kicked me out of his utility room. In July of 2004, I was standing outside a Holiday Inn in Reno. The summer heat had soared past 100 degrees. My entire existence, from waking to collapsing, revolved around hustling spare change for my next can of beer or rock of crack. On good days, I made enough to slip into the casinos, nurse the nickel slots, and hide in their air-conditioning. If luck struck, I could order a cheap hot dog and a bigger beer.

On one such afternoon, I actually won eighty bucks off a slot machine. I remember the adrenaline spike: Eighty bucks! That's a goldmine for someone living off scraps. My mind shot straight to, I can buy crack—ten-dollar rocks, one after another, enough to blitz my mind into oblivion for a day or more.

Back then, we street hustlers congregated around Cal Neva, drawn by its ninety-nine-cent breakfasts and dollar-fifty hot dog-and-beer combos. It was also ground zero for gossip: who was dealing where, which motel they used as their base, what girls were working a "stroll" that night. These details were currency; we were each other's Yelp reviews for every illegal transaction. And I was right in the thick of it, using my charm, wit, and connections to feed the habit that was slowly erasing my soul.

At some point that day, I ran into a stranger named Deshawn. He must've noticed my little slot-machine windfall because he sidled up, asked for a beer, and offered to help me score crack. I was naive enough—or simply too high—to think we were on friendly terms. But maybe I said the wrong thing, or maybe he saw me as an easy mark. The next thing I knew, I was waking up on the asphalt, head throbbing, tears of pain flooding my eyes. Apparently, he'd sucker-punched me so hard I blacked out. Some acquaintances rallied around me, but I was left with a broken jaw.

Washoe Medical Center took me in. The X-rays showed my jaw had shattered, needing plates and screws to lock it in place. The doctors gave me Percocet for the pain, along with a direct order: heal up, stay safe. In a fair world, that would have been a turning point. But in the real world—my world—things got worse.

After leaving the hospital, I landed a spot in a shelter for domestic violence survivors. It was a bizarre arrangement, but it meant a roof over my head. The rule was simple: no drugs, no booze, be in by curfew. I blew it within days. My jaw still wired shut, I found myself smoking crack in some stranger's motel room. Another argument. Another fist to my face. Another ambulance ride. Another surgery. My jaw was now broken a second time, the fresh wires and arch bars clenching me in torment. But even that didn't stop me from smoking.

At that point, I looked like a Frankenstein experiment—wires in my jaw, bruises on my cheeks, no stable place to sleep, no socks, no underwear, just battered sneakers and a T-shirt. I'd rely on random men for mini-lifelines—a beer here, a bed there. For a while, I'd even had a "sugar daddy," Eugene, who let me crash at his place. I wasn't gay, but I performed whatever he needed in exchange for the safety of four walls and maybe a meal. Then Eugene left town. And I sank further.

By the time I stumbled into that utility closet, I was convinced I'd never see 2005. Something in me had gone numb—except the raw, drilling pain of my jaw. The crack gave me fleeting relief, but as soon as the high dipped, the depression was back, deeper than ever.

Providence

I trace my moment of grace to September 22, 2004, the day the police tackled me in a Quik Mart parking lot. It was sheer irony: I'd finally decided I might go to Seattle for free treatment. My adoptive mother, Irene, had actually answered my desperate phone call—after all I'd done to her—and agreed to buy me a one-way bus ticket. I was due to leave that evening. All I needed was a few extra bucks for food during the 48-hour Greyhound ride.

I still had a single rock of crack in my pocket, and for one of the only times in my life, I didn't smoke it. Instead, I decided to sell it. Let me say that again: I was a chronic user with a pipe in hand day and night, yet I was about to hand that rock to someone else. Could that have been divine intervention? Who knows. But I approached a car in the Quik Mart lot that, in hindsight, screamed undercover. I handed the driver the rock. Took the twenty. Turned away. And then —sirens, shouting, hands pulling me down onto scorching asphalt.

Oddly enough, I felt this jolt of something close to relief.

Sure, I was being arrested for drug distribution—again. But I understood the unspoken outcome: I was going back to prison. And prison meant I was going to live. I'd survived behind bars before. In jail, you can't chain-smoke crack every day. In jail, your body has a chance (however brutal the environment might be) to break the cycle. In jail, a person might even find clarity.

So when the officer asked me why I was crying—I was sobbing like a lost child in the midday sun—I couldn't quite explain: *I'm crying because you saved my life, sir.* That was the truth. I knew if I'd walked freely another 24 hours, I'd have smoked or drunk myself to death. Or ended up as someone's punching bag again, maybe on the sidewalk, mouth parted in a final gasp. Instead, I was handcuffed and on my way to another cell.

The Price of Hope

Looking back, some might say that was my "rock bottom." But truth be told, I'd had more bottoms than I could count—days of near starvation, weeks in missions, peddling stolen goods, losing the trust of everyone I ever loved. If you'd asked me at any moment in that quagmire whether there was a future version of Ken—a version who'd stand on a stage, wearing a suit, raising millions of dollars for nonprofits, guiding other Black men toward redemption—I would've laughed in your face.

Yet that's what happened. That arrest in the Quik Mart parking lot began a pivot. Over time, I learned to harness the same fear, cunning, and energy I once used to hustle crack deals into fueling my recovery. Over time, I reconnected with my mother in a way that was more honest than I'd ever been, even if I'd stolen from her before. Over time, I confronted the humiliations of my childhood, the orphaned boy inside me who'd always felt less-than—and realized I could forgive that boy for the havoc he'd caused.

All that took years—prison stints, multiple attempts at sobriety, stumbles into old traps. But as I stand here writing these words, it's been nearly two decades since I surrendered to the police on that blazing Reno asphalt. I haven't touched a drug or had a drink since.

Why Am I Telling You This?

This story isn't some parade of shame or a cautionary tale that says, "Look how bad I was; don't be me." It's about the truth that no hole is too deep—even if you're half-buried. Maybe you aren't an addict, but you've messed up in other ways. Maybe you've battered your own sense of worth with heartbreak, or you feel stuck in a job that's draining your soul, or you're wearing a mask in a life that's never matched the dream you once had. The specifics differ, but the despair is the same.

My time living beneath brooms and roaches taught me that despair thrives in silence. It grows when you're too ashamed to admit where you are—or too convinced that no one would understand. But ironically, the more you speak the truth, the more you find out how many people carry burdens just like yours.

In the chapters that follow, I'm going to give you a raw, unfiltered account of how a bright, wide-eyed Dartmouth kid transformed into a homeless prostitute, then reemerged as a nonprofit leader and dedicated mentor. You'll see the heartbreak and betrayal—particularly the betrayal of my own potential. You'll see the near-misses: overdoses, violent fights, jail, and experiences that nearly cost me my life. You'll see glimpses of grace—my mother's love, the kindness of near-strangers, and that intangible something that kept me from giving up.

I hope you see yourself, or someone you love, reflected here. Not in every detail, but in the underlying thread: that you can slip from promise to peril in shockingly few steps. And that you can climb back up, one shaky step at a time.

A Lifelong Search for Belonging

Let's be honest about one more thing: no one sets out to ruin their life. We're all searching for love, acceptance, or that blissful sense of belonging. I sure was. A giant chunk of my identity hinged on wanting people to say, *"Ken, you're smart, you're special, we like you."* At Dartmouth, I found a community of high achievers—but I also found that I didn't quite fit the preppy mold. My father had hammered into me that I wasn't good enough. Combine that with a campus brimming with top-shelf liquor, unlimited parties, and a sense that every night was a new adventure, and you get a deadly cocktail for a kid with a hungry heart.

As you'll read, fear of rejection fueled many of my bad decisions. So did anger—anger at my father for not loving me right, anger at my mother for not always protecting me, anger at the world for shining so brightly on everyone else. Crack offered me a suspension of that anger. For 30 minutes, I could feel unstoppable. Then, a crushing low would drop me deeper than before. Rinse and repeat for two decades.

Becoming Ken

If I had to pinpoint the single greatest challenge on my journey, it wasn't quitting crack or facing prison. It was surviving my own self: the man who lied to people he loved, the man who betrayed his own mother, the man who used women, men—anyone—to fill a bottomless void. This book is about how I finally started to love Ken—how I forgave him—and how that self-love freed me to truly connect with others.

"Becoming Ken" is both the name of my darkest struggle and a testament to the fact that I'm still here, typing these words, excited for tomorrow. You might question how it's possible to forgive yourself after the pain you've caused. Trust me, I asked the same question. But I found the more I turned my experiences into service—helping raise money for nonprofits, mentoring young men to avoid my path—the more I realized that every wound carried a lesson. And that lesson could be a lifeline for someone else.

Where We Go From Here

In the following chapters, we'll travel from the day I stepped onto Dartmouth's picturesque campus—full of naive optimism—through the slow descent into addiction, the hustling culture in Reno, violent confrontations, and the humiliations of being an educated Black man sleeping in a broom closet. Along the way, I'll show you the father who tried to kill my mother, the mother who survived bullet wounds and eventually found her own brand of resilience, and the near-angelic souls who offered me grace when I deserved none.

We'll arrive at the story of how I discovered my birth mother—the woman I never knew—and how that puzzle piece completed a chunk of my identity. Finally, I'll walk you through the hard-won truths that allowed me not just to get sober, but to find a life where I genuinely thrive.

If you stay with me for this ride, you won't get some neatly wrapped fairytale. I'm not tying a bow around my trauma to claim it was all "worth it." I was a criminal, I was an addict, I was a menace to the people who loved me. But I did the work, and I found a path to become a man who helps others, who stands upright—still scarred, still flawed, but free.

Final Word Before We Begin

I want you to understand the depth of my gratitude as I share these pages with you. Gratitude for my mom, Irene, who answered my call. Gratitude for the Reno PD officers who pinned me to the asphalt that day. Gratitude for every single counselor, sponsor, friend, and even the enemies who reminded me I wasn't done yet.

I hope you'll see that wherever you are in your journey—dorm room, mission bunk, corporate suite, or that broom closet you never asked for—there's a space for redemption. Real life doesn't always allow neat second chances, but it does allow for personal revolutions.

When you've finished reading, you might realize we all have a version of that September 22 waiting somewhere in our story. We all have a choice—hide from it or face it, own up to it, maybe even embrace it. Because often, it's in the hardest collisions that we finally find ourselves.

So let's step inside. Let me show you how the dream turned into a nightmare, and how that nightmare coughed up something precious: the possibility of becoming a better man.

Turn the page. I'll start with the vantage point of a young Ken Miller, eyes wide, stepping onto Dartmouth's campus. You'll see hope, fear, and a lethal obsession with being liked. You'll see the seeds of my future unraveling. But I promise: keep walking with me, and you'll also see how, at the darkest brink, a door labeled "Redemption" was waiting. And how—by grace or grit—I found the courage to push it open.

Let's begin.

PART ONE
FROM IVY LEAGUE DREAMS TO THE EDGE

CHAPTER 1
A BRIGHT BEGINNING

For nearly two decades, I celebrated my birthday on October 15 because that's what I was always told. It wasn't until I was in my late teens that I learned from my official birth certificate that I was actually born at 11:01 p.m. on October 15, 1962, in Long Island, New York. At birth, my given name was Kenneth John Horne.

I'd known since I was three or four that I was a foster kid, and by five, I knew I didn't have a real mom. I can't pinpoint the exact moment that realization hit—it was just an understanding that sat in my chest like a dull ache. My younger brother, Jacob, and I had been shuffled from one foster home to another, sometimes every few weeks, sometimes every couple of months. We were the same age. No one told us we were twins, but I latched on to it the moment someone mentioned it. It felt right. He was my other half, and for a while, we moved in unison—together against whatever the world threw our way.

I recall one of the countless foster homes we lived in,

where a Ford Mustang pulled up to fetch us. A woman in her mid-twenties (maybe early thirties) got out, told us to gather our few belongings, and off we went yet again. That was just the routine: pack, leave, drive off to some unknown place because the last one decided we weren't the right fit. But I had Jacob, and he had me.

We landed at the home of John and Olive Turley when I was five. I remember stepping inside, feeling the warmth of a lived-in house filled with plump, good-natured, Southern Black folks. They treated us with a kind of affection we hadn't seen before. The Turleys already had a ten-year-old son, Mark, who became a big-brother figure in no time. I even started calling myself Kenneth John Horne Turley. I never wanted to leave.

Jacob and I stuck together every second—until September 1967, when we started kindergarten. Out of nowhere, I learned I wouldn't be in the same classroom with him. I didn't understand why he had to go somewhere else. It felt as if the universe had yanked my heart out of my chest. I later heard the grown-ups call him "retarded," that older, hurtful term we now replace with "developmentally disabled." I couldn't see anything different about him. All I knew was that my best friend, my twin in spirit, was separated from me. I hated the feeling of being alone. Jacob had always been the one I woke up next to, the one I fell asleep with. And all at once, that steady sense of belonging was tested.

The Moment Everything Changed

Meanwhile, Samuel and Irene Miller were sitting in the Windham Adoption Agency (later known as Graham Windham), hoping to adopt a Black child. It was the 1960s, and even for an African American couple, adopting a Black child was neither cheap nor easy. Irene especially longed for a son, having never had children of her own. Sam had two kids from a prior marriage, but they were already grown and out in the world. Our paths were about to collide in the most unexpected way.

I remember standing at the Turleys' window one day, watching Jacob playing outside because I was stuck indoors for doing something naughty. The song "Get Ready" by The Temptations played somewhere in my head:

I'm bringing you a love that's true
So get ready, so get ready...

There's no telling why certain details burn themselves into our memory. Maybe it's the power of music. Maybe it's because a day or two later, Mrs. Turley pulled me aside, saying, "There's a nice couple here who want to spend time with just you." Every instinct screamed that I couldn't leave Jacob, but at the same time, every fiber of my little being yearned for the kind of mother-love I'd never truly known.

Sam and Irene Miller visited me off and on for a few weeks. Irene, who would soon become "Mom," exuded warmth that made me believe all those daydreams about having a mother. Over time, she told me that she'd found my picture almost by chance: it slipped out of a file while she and Sam flipped through photos of adoptable children. She saw my face, looked at Sam, and said, "I want this child."

I didn't know much about Sam during those first meetings. I only sensed his quiet anger—a tension simmering just below the surface. But that day in the courthouse, when I stood before the judge at age six and he asked if I wanted Sam and Irene as my parents, I answered without hesitation. Yes, I wanted a mother, and if Sam came with her, so be it.

And so, in 1968, I became Kenneth John Horne Turley Miller. My adoption was legally "closed," meaning I had no details about my birth parents beyond that single hint on my new birth certificate. I had a new last name, a new home in upstate New York, and a brand-new mother's love. Yet losing Jacob felt like amputating half my soul. I was thrilled to have Irene, but I still cried for my brother.

Loving Irene

Mom poured her heart into me from day one. When she realized I couldn't read, couldn't tell time, and couldn't tie my shoes, she refused to let me stagnate. An accomplished nurse, an intellectual, a dancer, and a poet, she had the determination to match her degrees. She'd studied at Hunter College, earned multiple master's degrees from Columbia Teachers College, and was unstoppable in anything she tackled.

In a single summer, the gap in my reading skills closed. She wrote sounds on index cards, drilled me on phonics, and listened patiently while I stuttered through syllables. Day by day, she was my anchor, and I soaked up her attention like a sponge. Perhaps I learned to love reading so intensely because it gave me the one-on-one time I desperately craved with her.

But it wasn't all idyllic. Sam hovered in the background: stoic, watchful, carrying a deep well of discontent. He was a WWII veteran—a Black man who'd faced segregation in the Army and used alcohol to numb old wounds. He worked as an accountant, but mostly I remember how he'd scowl and shift whenever I got too much of Irene's attention.

Eventually, Sam's resentment turned to anger, and anger turned to violence. I quickly learned to fear him in a way I had never feared anyone else. He was like a ticking bomb—unpredictable, except that I always knew he was ticking.

Surviving School—And Sam

Back then, rural schools were tiny outposts with a single classroom per grade. By second grade, I had a sixth-grade reading level—but my report cards also carried big red U's (Unsatisfactory) for behavior. I was bored, I acted out, and my mother's gentle discipline didn't scare me one bit. The minute she threatened, "I'll tell your dad," though, my heart pounded in terror. Sam was the last person I wanted my mischief reported to.

I remember being in third grade when he stormed into my classroom for the first time. The teacher's supply closet door swung open, and there he was, looming silently. My stomach dropped. My classmates looked around, confused, but I was frozen in dread. I'd never seen him so sober and so angry all at once—and especially not in front of witnesses. He said, "Let's go," and I obeyed without a word.

Sober or drunk, Sam was a man of few words. Drunk, though, he was something else—a swirl of self-pity, quiet rage, and apricot brandy. He drank in his car on his day off. If I wasn't careful stepping off the school bus, I might find him awake, waiting to unleash a twisted chore or interrogation on me. If he was passed out, I could slink into the house quietly. Either way, every Wednesday brought the same knot of fear in my chest.

A Cycle of Hiding and Hoping

Many nights, Mom and I fled to a motel, letting Sam stew in his own anger. She'd wait for him to sober up, accept his half-hearted apologies, and then we'd return. Each time, I hoped it might be different, though deep down, I knew it wouldn't. He was at war with himself—and with me.

I tried to make sense of it all. I was bright, curious, hungry for love and acceptance. But Sam's presence overshadowed that craving—my days filled with attempts to dodge his random punishments and humiliations. Once, he forced me to chop down a little grove of saplings with a chainsaw twice my size while he stood back, arms folded, glaring. The sight of those spindly trees whipping back at me, the saw blade jerking in my wobbly hands, haunts me even now. It was as if he were challenging fate to slice my limbs off.

Still, I was a child clinging to any scraps of normalcy I could find: Cub Scouts, collecting candy for friends, burying my face in books. But as I got older, my longing for real friendship led me to steal money from Mom's purse so I could buy kids' loyalty with sweets. I desperately wanted to be liked. I had to be.

I got caught, of course. That fiasco ended with me staying four months in Detroit with Aunt Pauline, allowing me to breathe free of Sam. It was a strange relief I didn't question—just a chance to live without constant fear. But the lesson that "friendship can be bought" stayed with me, sowing seeds of complicated relationships later.

A Brief Reprieve: Alaska

By seventh grade, Sam's drinking became unbearable again, so Mom pulled us out of New York altogether. She landed a new job as Dean of the Nursing Program at Anchorage Community College in Alaska, where she'd earn far more than she ever did in New York. Just before my 13th birthday, we packed whatever we could salvage from our ravaged home and left.

For a few months in 1975, I tasted real freedom. We lived in an overpriced, cramped Anchorage apartment (prices skyrocketed during the Alaska pipeline construction), but we were at peace. No Sam, no fists, no terror. I walked around starry-eyed at the snowy mountains, made new friends, and listened to Mom sing in the evenings. It was heaven.

Until December, when Sam began calling, pleading for a

second chance. Mom asked if I'd let him come. I begged her, "Don't do it." But cultural, marital, and emotional ties bound her to him. She said yes.

For a while, it was calm. He even found a job at an oil company, and they bought a house in Chester Valley. For the first time, I went to a school where I wasn't the only Black kid. I discovered classic R&B, plus a ton of other music—I was equally enthralled by Led Zeppelin and Fleetwood Mac. I'd saved up for a Sears Quadraphonic stereo, which was my treasure. I spent weekends making mix tapes and daydreaming about the future.

High School Success and Hidden Battles

Bartlett High School became my launchpad. I joined sports, excelled in classes, nailed AP exams, and got recruitment letters from over a hundred colleges. My mother's academic rigor took root in me. We shared an unspoken vow: I would do better, go further, become something big. I had no interest in drugs or alcohol—Sam's example repelled me from both—and I remained a virgin the whole time, unsure of how to handle intimacy.

But senior year brought tension back. Sam's drinking flared anew. Fear scuttled beneath my everyday successes, overshadowing any pride I felt. Then something else rocked me: Mom told me she had information about my birth mother—a teenage white girl. The revelation shattered everything I'd assumed. I'd pictured a Black woman who looked like Irene, and now that image collapsed. Part of me fumed at this unknown white girl who had "discarded" me. Anger smoldered, and I had nowhere to aim it.

I retreated further into the safe spaces I had: good grades, music, and reading. I applied to a few Ivy League schools plus my beloved Oberlin, ultimately choosing Dartmouth College. My mother was proud, and I was...well, I was a ball of nerves. Because even with my acceptance letter in hand, I was still an unsure teenage kid who feared the sound of a certain drunk man's footsteps.

The Final Eruption

One late afternoon during my senior year, Sam found *The Pearl*, a risqué Victorian-era pornography collection I'd hidden under my bed. Furious, he called me a "faggot" and demanded I stand up while he spoke. Something snapped in me. I swung at him, a raw reflex—my first real blow. A twisted half-smile flickered across his face, like he'd waited forever for me to challenge him.

We fought viciously. My mother dialed the cops, screaming. Sam pinned me down, unleashing years of pent-up rage in each punch. The police arrived, and Mom and I left. This time, she filed a restraining order. She chose my safety over him at last, a stand that was both liberating and heartbreaking for her.

I spent the final months of my senior year hiding in another cramped apartment, walking to school with eyes scanning the streets in case Sam jumped out of some alley. At graduation, I was smiling on the outside—honors student, scholarship kid—but inside, I was bruised and exhausted.

In the fall of 1980, I was seventeen and left for Dartmouth, carrying with me a swirl of unspoken pain, a thirst for motherly love, a fear that I wasn't good enough, and a reluctant wonder about who I truly was beyond the name Kenneth John Horne Turley Miller.

Looking Ahead

My childhood had ended up being the dawn of a long struggle—wherein a bright-minded, mother-hungry kid from New York and Alaska faced a father's tyranny, a brother's disappearance, and the brewing questions of race and identity. As a young man, I had stepped onto the Ivy League campus of Dartmouth, hoping for a fresh start. But, as you'll see, I took every buried fear, every old wound, and every secret longing with me. Survival had become my specialty, but there's a whole world beyond just surviving.

From the crisp halls of an Ivy League campus to the darker, drug-fueled streets, where even deeper trials awaited. Because while punching Sam was one milestone. It didn't set me free—Not yet. I was on a collision course with my own undiscovered addictions, illusions, and heartbreaks—each step bringing me closer to a choice. Would I stay broken?...Or fight for a life that matched my mother's unwavering belief in me?

CHAPTER 1: MY REFLECTIONS

The early pieces of my life—foster homes, a father's anger, and a mother's hopeful love—laid the groundwork for both my resilience and my deepest wounds. It's easy to look at childhood chaos and assume you'll outgrow it. But I learned, sometimes painfully, that what happens in those formative years can echo through everything that follows. Recognizing how adoption, fear, and longing shaped me was the first step toward healing, even if I didn't fully understand it at the time.

1. **Longing for Family Runs Deep** - Don't underestimate the power of wanting to belong. From moving foster homes to finally landing with the Millers, I realized that a child's heart will latch onto any promise of love. If you're still trying to fill that hole, be honest about what you're seeking—and why.
2. **A Fractured Home Leaves Hidden Scars** - My father's anger and unpredictability taught me fear before I learned trust. Those scars don't vanish just because you grow up. If you've walked through an abusive or unstable home, remember you may still carry that hurt. Facing it is tough, but denial only cements the damage.

3. **Identity Can Be Complex—and Confusing** - Learning my birth mother was white rattled my sense of who I was. Identity isn't always a simple box to check. Give yourself space to explore the pieces of your story, whether cultural, racial, or personal, without shame.
4. **Fear Shapes Behavior More Than We Realize** - Even as a little boy, I tried to buy friendships with stolen money—I was that desperate for acceptance. If you notice yourself going to extremes for approval, ask: "What fear is driving this?" Underneath most self-sabotage lies a deep-seated anxiety about rejection or abandonment.
5. **You Can't Outrun the Past** - My mother and I fled Sam's outbursts, even moving to Alaska, but the emotional fallout never stayed behind. Changing locations or circumstances won't solve the root. Find ways—therapy, support groups, trusted mentors—to address what you're running from.

CHAPTER 2
CRACKS IN THE FOUNDAITON

Dartmouth College can easily be described as one of the most beautiful campuses in the United States, ranking alongside the University of Virginia or parts of Cornell in scenic splendor. Nestled in the Upper Valley, Dartmouth's rural charm greets you the moment you catch sight of its stately halls and wide green lawns. Mountain ranges in the distance stand guard like old sentinels, and the campus itself appears as a perfectly staged painting that changes with each of New England's four seasons. Autumn at Dartmouth shines most notably—brilliant oranges, fiery reds, and glowing yellows paint the campus under crisp skies. You feel a collective invitation to explore the trails, cheer on the football team, or simply amble along the campus green, taking in the life and color all around.

Yet, amid the majestic setting, I was aware that many things lay just beyond my emotional and intellectual preparation—especially how deeply alone I would feel after leaving home. In my mind, I'd told myself there would be challenges, but I hadn't anticipated a certain churning in my stomach that kept asking, *Do I really belong here?* Beneath my excitement about escaping the fear-ridden house of my father, a quiet dread lived inside me, whispering that this new environment might simply be another place to feel unsteady, out of place, and alone.

First Impressions

I arrived on campus in the fall of 1980, feeling equal parts relief and apprehension. Relief that I was now thousands of miles away from Sam's outbursts, away from the oppressive tension of that home in Anchorage. Apprehension because, as I define fear, it's the future anticipation or expectation of pain—and a big part of me was braced for a pain I couldn't yet name. Perhaps it was the possibility of failing or of being exposed as an impostor in this high-achieving world. Or maybe it was the looming dread of not finding genuine friends. Whatever label it deserved, the swirling sense of not belonging coursed through me from day one.

Those first days on campus were a blur of orientation events, placement tests, and social invitations that left me feeling both thrilled and overwhelmed. The notion of "Minority Special" placement tests, as many of the incoming minority students called them, hit me almost immediately. Dartmouth wanted to evaluate the readiness of students—particularly those recruited to diversify the school—and funnel them into the level of math, English, or science that matched their background. I discovered quickly that my liberal-arts strengths didn't translate well in math and sciences. While my English test placements were good, the math side of me needed a remedial track just to catch up. In a single stroke, my academic confidence took a blow. I realized I wasn't quite the star student I'd believed myself to be in high school—and the old creeping thought returned: *Ken, you don't really fit here.*

Meanwhile, I couldn't help noticing how others slipped seamlessly into the Dartmouth scene. Many of my classmates came from elite prep schools—places like Phillips Exeter, Miss Porter's, or Andover—and carried themselves with a practiced ease in academic discussions. They wore pressed khakis, had boat shoes, and talked about their parents' country club weekends. I came from Anchorage, Alaska, with a father who terrified me, a mother who believed in me, and a public high school that offered minimal depth in math and science. It wasn't lost on me how wide that gap was.

An Invitation to Belong

The first evening I walked into Brown Hall, dragging a suitcase of clothes and sparse belongings, I passed a door propped open. Inside, several guys lounged on the floor, unpacking, sipping from bottles, and passing around a joint. Their laughter spilled into the hallway. The rich smell of marijuana made my nostrils flare. One of them flashed a big grin and motioned for me to come in. For a moment, I stood there, heart pounding at the idea of using illegal substances in my first hour on campus. I mumbled an excuse—"I'll catch you guys later," or something equally vague—and ducked away, anxious not to ruin my entire college career before it began. The same naive part of me flashed on an image: me being hauled off by campus security, or maybe even the police. Up to that point in life, I'd had half a beer once. I was a small-town kid, a virgin, underage, with a father who drank himself senseless—and, ironically, I still barely touched alcohol. But it was clear Dartmouth's social culture would revolve around weekend parties, Greek life events, and no shortage of "vices"—or, as many might say, no shortage of ways to let off steam.

I soon discovered that letting off steam or "cutting loose" at Dartmouth was more an everyday phenomenon than a weekend treat. The intensity of the coursework combined with everyone's desire to fit in made partying an immediate draw. A subtle pressure hovered: If you're not at these gatherings, you're invisible.

The Subtleties of Preppy Culture

I began noticing some campus hallmarks that set me apart. For starters, the fashion culture. Groups of parents paraded around in matching lime-green-and-pink golf pants, like some bizarre uniform that screamed, *We've got this place locked down.* Their kids roamed the dorms in penny loafers, Polos with the collars popped, appearing to have stepped straight from a high-end magazine spread. I wasn't entirely clueless about how to dress, but I owned maybe two or three shirts that might pass the Dartmouth "prep test." A deep sense of envy hit me whenever I saw those entire families so put-together. Where was my family? My mother, Irene, was supportive from afar, but no cluster of stylish relatives strolled campus with me that first weekend.

Just as tellingly, many of these students had been prepping for college from kindergarten onward—SAT tutors, advanced science labs, AP classes since sophomore year. Meanwhile, I'd been dealing with a father whose brand of "extracurricular activity" involved drunken confrontations and skirmishes over leftover food bowls. My high school, though it served me as well as it could, didn't catapult me into advanced calculus or college-level vocabulary. So academically, I felt behind, forced to make up ground at every turn. Emotionally, the gap was even larger: they radiated certainty. I radiated anxiety.

And yet, I also saw an opening. I realized quickly there were fraternities, clubs, and social circles where I might claim some form of membership. The lure of Greek life was strong. At Dartmouth, fraternities were integral to social standing—some with storied histories, some known for raucous parties, some with academic prestige, and some with more progressive, inclusive vibes. By the second or third week of the quarter, I'd visited a few fraternity houses just to see the culture for myself. And it was exactly as you'd expect: loud music, easy booze, and plenty of flirting with the visiting "Ivy Sisters," as the out-of-town college women were sometimes called—those from Smith, Wellesley, Holyoke. To my teenage eyes, fraternities looked like giant parties with a built-in family you got to choose. And I craved that sense of family.

My mother, being the disciplined, academically focused presence in my life, had warned me not to pledge in my freshman year. But the desire to belong tugged at me almost nightly—particularly when I walked by houses like Bones Gate (informally known as BG) or Alpha Delta and heard cheering, smelled the beer, and caught glimpses of the arms-thrown-over-the-shoulder camaraderie. Once more, I asked myself, "Where else can I fit in if not there?" It was a question that haunted me like an echo through the deserted corridors of a new school, where half the faces already seemed to know each other and the other half seemed content in their own corners.

Seeds of Addiction

A major shift in my life was happening beneath the surface—like a sinkhole forming slowly, hollowing out the ground. If you'd asked me then, I'd have told you I was fine, if a bit lonely. But in truth, the deeper fear was that I would be exposed: exposed as academically less prepared, exposed as a kid with a father who drank himself into brutality, exposed as someone whose mother left everything behind just to keep him safe. That fear of exposure fed a hunger for acceptance. I was new to being on my own, new to seeing free-flowing booze in hallways, new to witnessing open marijuana use among my peers. A small, quiet voice said: *Maybe you should do what they do so you won't stand out as a prude or an outcast.*

Another part of me, the resentful part that had grown up under Sam's violent, drunken episodes, loathed the very smell of alcohol. Why would I choose something that had nearly destroyed my youth?

That war within me—an unconscious tilt between *I hate alcohol* and *I hate being left out*—set the stage for my own complicated relationship with substances. Although I didn't take the first drink that fall, I'd planted a seed of curiosity. Every party, every passing whiff of weed or open cup of punch reminded me that inclusion might be just a few sips or puffs away. I started showing up sometimes, not to indulge heavily, but to be physically present. The social energy in those spaces felt electric. There were upperclassmen who would slap me on the back and say, "Lighten up, Ken, have fun!" And the thought of letting go—if only to forget how "behind" I was in math, or how alone I felt—was appealing in ways I only half-understood.

I also noticed how no one asked me detailed questions about my background. If they inquired about home, I'd say I was from Anchorage, Alaska, that my mother was a nurse educator, and my father was "a professional accountant." I'd gloss right over the darker truths. Tucking away my real story allowed me to present a polished, palatable version of myself. *He's the academically capable, mild-mannered freshman from the wilds of Alaska—how charming.* The performance of belonging came with a price, though. Each time I withheld how I felt or pretended to be more confident than I was, the tension in me grew. I was basically building a structure with cracks already in its foundation.

Dartmouth's Social Hierarchy

Fitting in at Dartmouth also meant dealing with an unmistakable hierarchy, with old-money legacies at the top. They walked around campus with last names that matched dorms or libraries. They'd greet each other: "Hey, Vanderbilt!" or "See you at tennis, Armstrong!" I'd just nod quietly, painfully aware I wasn't part of that multi-generational tradition. Then there was the middle echelon—students from well-to-do families or top-tier public schools who had enough social capital to join certain clubs or excel academically without missing a beat. At the bottom—though it wasn't an official ranking system—were those of us from less-privileged backgrounds, often minority students or scholarship kids, trying to hack through the academic rigors and unspoken social codes. I was nowhere near the top of that pyramid, and I felt it.

On top of everything, the early 1980s was still a time when the presence of Black students at Dartmouth was considered "groundbreaking." A small community of us came from a scattering of places: big cities, Africa, the Caribbean. A few might have been from suburban enclaves or well-known private schools. We'd gather at the Afro-Am House, or wave to each other on campus with that small nod of recognition. We came in different stripes—some hyper-involved in Black Student Union activities, others, like me, a bit uncertain whether we fit among the Black activism crowd given our backgrounds. There was also a subtle expectation from the administration that we'd unify, but the truth was we were as diverse internally as the entire college. Even in that group, I sometimes felt not Black enough—I listened to Led Zeppelin and revered classic rock as much as I did Earth, Wind & Fire.

All of this internal friction—cultural, academic, social—played into the earliest seeds of my addictive tendencies. While I wasn't yet throwing back beers nightly, the impulse to numb or to "do something" was quietly sprouting. *I can't keep living in this halfway authenticity,* I'd think. *But how do I change it?*

Bones Gate and Fogcutters

By the middle of my freshman year, I'd started hearing tales of legendary frat parties. Bones Gate (BG) was one of the most storied, known for diversity in membership but also a reputation for unstoppable partying. A friend—someone who saw my social unease—dragged me to a BG house gathering one night. It was overwhelming in every sense: the roar of music, the crush of bodies, the open bar, the distinct smell of spilled beer and sweat. Groups of guys wearing the BG letters introduced themselves, hammered out jokes, and high-fived girls from Wellesley or Holyoke who'd driven in for the night. The air felt thick with hedonistic glee. They talked about "Fogcutters," a signature BG tradition—some sort of potent punch and wild theme party that overshadowed most other fraternities. At that moment, no one cared I was a freshman or that I felt academically insecure. They just said, "Grab a cup, man. Let's have a good time."

And for the first time, I almost caved on my vow. I stared

at the frothy red mixture swirling in the plastic cup. *Why not?* some rebellious corner of me urged. "You only live once," someone said, handing me the cup. *Yes, and I saw what that 'once' looked like for my father,* I thought, the memory of Sam's brandy-soaked rampages burning in my mind. So I put the cup down and forced a grin, muttering something about "needing to pace myself." People moved on—there were plenty of others who'd take the offered drink. That small act of refusal felt like a victory. I was proud of not giving in, but also, in the afterglow of that party, a whisper of alienation surfaced again: *If I keep saying no forever, will I ever be embraced as a 'real brother'?*

Emotional Triggers

Even in those first few months, phone calls from my mother underlined how precarious my well-being was. She'd ask how classes were going, whether I'd found any close friends, if I'd been studying enough. I told her I was doing fine. We never directly addressed Sam or the havoc he'd left behind. Sometimes I sensed she wanted to ask: *Are you staying away from trouble? Are you truly okay?* But she also knew I was forging a new life and that she couldn't protect me from across the country. The fewer details I shared, the less she worried. Or so I thought.

While I might not have been conscious of it then, each phone call or letter from home nudged an old wound. I'd think of the fear I fled in Anchorage, how Sam's fists or belt once determined my day. In that light, the promise of a "safe" kind of intoxication—the sort my classmates indulged in for pure social ease—didn't look so bad. At least they were laughing, not swinging belts. *I can handle a little buzz without turning into Sam,* I'd reassure myself. Step by step, rationalization set in. My mother, if she'd known, would have asked me to find better ways to handle stress. She would have pointed out that I was ignoring the underlying terror of rejection. But I was determined to prove to everyone—my father especially—that I could succeed on my own terms.

The cracks in my foundation, though, were definitely widening. I recognized that behind the neat dorm exteriors and the glossy campus brochures, a shadow side existed. *A student can vanish into anonymity here,* my darker thoughts insisted, *and no one will notice until it's too late.* I had no idea how literal that foreshadowing might become in the years to follow. For now, I drifted, half-participating in social events, half-committing to academic demands, and wholly certain that I must not let slip how insecure I felt.

Uncertain Future

By the end of my freshman year at Dartmouth, I was still grappling with a swirling mix of excitement, longing, and emotional tumult. The college was everything it promised—gorgeous, historically significant, academically challenging—and yet, for me, it was also a place of simmering disquiet. I was forging friendships in fraternities that celebrated partying as ritual. I was nursing anxieties over my academic preparedness. And most crucially, I was staying silent about the depth of my father's effect on me—his addiction, rage, and the battered sense of self I carried. It's not that I saw myself as an emerging addict. The idea never crossed my mind, given how lightly I drank that year. But looking back, I see how each emotional trigger and each unspoken secret was piling up like kindling, awaiting a spark.

If my bright beginning at Dartmouth was the outer facade, those cracks in the foundation were already spider-webbing beneath. The seeds of addiction—my longing for acceptance, my battered sense of identity, the silent trauma from home—had been planted. And, as with every seed, it only took the right conditions to grow roots and break the surface. The story of how that happened would evolve in the chapters ahead—where partying transformed into genuine self-medication, and simple academic or social pressure gave way to an all-consuming need to numb.

Looking back on that first year, I can still taste the mixture of hope and dread. Hope that I'd find my place in a privileged world, dread that I'd never truly belong. And as always, fear—the future anticipation of pain—loomed. I clung to the belief that I could skirt around it if I was careful enough. But sometimes, the only way to deal with a sinkhole is not to tiptoe around its edges, but to face its collapse head-on.

CHAPTER 2: MY REFLECTIONS

Stepping onto Dartmouth's campus felt like crossing into a new world—privileged, picturesque, and buzzing with opportunity. Part of me believed it could wash away the fear and trauma I'd carried. But I quickly discovered that no amount of scenic beauty or social prestige can fix what's broken inside you. Instead, I found myself juggling the pressure to fit in with the weight of my own secrets. Those cracks in my foundation started to widen the moment I tried to patch them with external validation.

1. **New Surroundings Don't Guarantee a Fresh Start** - Leaving home was a relief, but the old wounds—my father's abuse, my lingering insecurities—came with me. Relocating can bring hope, yet true change requires confronting the baggage you've packed.
2. **Acceptance at Any Cost Can Be Dangerous** - I was willing to do almost anything to feel like I belonged, whether that meant lurking around frat parties or forcing myself into someone else's comfort zone. If you're bending over backward for approval, pay attention. Your authentic self might be getting lost in the process.

3. **Early Warnings of Addiction** - Even though I wasn't yet fully hooked on alcohol or drugs, the social scene planted seeds—my curiosity, my desire to numb insecurities, my fear of being left out. If you notice similar urges or rationalizations ("everyone else is doing it"), it's worth taking a step back to assess.
4. **Academic Pressure Can Mask Deeper Issues** - Falling behind in math or feeling outclassed by prep-school peers stung my pride, but the real problem was my sense of not measuring up as a person. If you find yourself obsessing over grades or work to avoid facing emotional pain, you may be treating a symptom instead of the root cause.
5. **Your Story Matters—Even If You Hide It** - I downplayed my background, acting like a typical freshman while carrying enormous weight inside. If you're telling half-truths about who you are or where you come from, it's a sign you might need support or a safe place to unpack your story. It's hard to heal what you keep in the dark.

CHAPTER 3
WHEN ILLUSIONS SPLINTER

My working definition of an alcoholic is someone who, once they start drinking, has no reliable ability to control how much they consume. Under alcohol's influence, this person makes crippling decisions—damaging not just themselves but also the people who care about them, and society at large. Webster's might say it more concisely, but after half a century of being an alcoholic myself, that's the gist I stand by: no control once you start and mounting, inevitable pain on the back end.

By the fall of my freshman year at Dartmouth, I'd moved from innocence to a fast, furious relationship with alcohol. In those early weeks, it felt like an extension of the campus party scene—everyone around me was drinking, so I reasoned I should join them. Where it truly turned dark was my willingness—even eagerness—to "rage." We used that term casually to describe heavy drinking—someone who drank until blackouts or kept going beyond any sense of safety. But for me, "rager" wasn't just a label; it was already my reality. By December of that first term, I was a full-fledged alcoholic, though I couldn't yet see the storms forming in my life.

Campus Pressures and A Double Life

I loved the camaraderie of my fraternity brothers or the guys who'd soon become my brothers. The parties gave me the feeling that every night, I had a family, an unspoken acceptance. At first, I clung to that like a life raft against the constant undercurrent of self-doubt. Despite pockets of success—C-level or better grades, surviving the "gut" classes, forging friendships—I felt the pressures of being a young Black man in a mostly white Ivy League environment. It felt as though I was living several lives at once:

- The academically challenged but still-capable student who slotted in last-minute papers and avoided class.
- The heavy-drinking fraternity pledge rapidly descending into dependency.
- The young man still dealing with father-induced traumas and an unstable sense of self.

These roles clashed constantly in my mind. On the outside, though, I likely appeared as another fun-loving undergrad who sometimes partied too hard.

Blackouts and "Missing" Pieces

Things worsened that spring. I started experiencing blackouts—entire nights disappearing from my memory. It wasn't just waking up with a headache; I'd learn the next day from someone else that I'd done something humiliating, unethical, or that I'd ended up somewhere I shouldn't have been. My shame ballooned each time I heard about my exploits the following morning. Occasionally, people laughed it off: "Wow, Ken, you were wild last night!" But privately, I felt more panic than pride. I didn't trust myself if a few drinks could vault me into oblivion.

The shame manifested in ways I'd later have to confront head-on. On some nights, for instance, I'd phone my high school girlfriend back in Alaska, mid-bender, and ramble for hours about nothing. She'd doze off, and I'd still be talking. Later, my mother would complain about these late-night bills—hundreds of dollars in long-distance charges I was powerless to pay. Yet none of these consequences stopped the cycle. I kept sinking deeper into the secrecy that always shadows addictive behavior.

Cocaine: A New Temptation

By freshman spring, my crowd introduced me to powder cocaine. I remember one fraternity brother we nicknamed "Hard Rock" offering it around. At first, cocaine seemed like just another Ivy League "experiment"—like LSD in the '60s or ecstasy in the '90s. Early '80s cocaine was marketed as non-addictive, glamorized by celebrities, athletes, and the disco scene. Most fraternities had at least a small group indulging, casually passing around lines on mirrors. If you didn't consider yourself an addict, it was just another party pastime. People were oblivious—willfully or otherwise—to the trouble it could become.

But for me, already losing battles with alcohol, cocaine was a gasoline-soaked match. My first couple of tries didn't deliver the immediate rush I'd anticipated, so I kept pushing, determined to ignite that euphoric spark. Soon, it wasn't me doing the drug; the drug was beginning to own me. For the rest of that spring, I indulged at every opportunity. It set a pattern: if beer or liquor lifted my mood, coke could keep me partying longer, sharper, and seemingly immune to a hang-over—until the inevitable crash. I convinced myself it was just normal college mischief, but the illusions were already starting to crack.

Confronting Father's Shadow

Each long break—winter, spring, or summer—brought the same dilemma: Where do I go? Frequent flights from New England to Alaska were often unaffordable, so I'd usually end up staying with relatives or friends on the East Coast. But sometimes I did return to Anchorage, which meant bracing for my father's lingering menace. Even if I didn't see him, the city itself was haunted by memories of his brandy-fueled rages and near escapes from his violence. That tension combined with my growing dependence on booze and cocaine made "home" a twisted place filled with resentment, uneasy love, and deepening denial.

Mom had found a semblance of happiness with Dennis, a white, blue-collar man she genuinely liked. Unlike Sam's angry presence, Dennis was gentle and kind. Yet, ironically, I resented sharing her affection. After years of living in my father's shadow, it felt foreign—and unsettling—to watch her finally be content. Any sense of calm clashed sharply with my own restlessness. I constantly yearned to return to Dartmouth and my fraternity brothers. At eighteen, I might have appeared halfway to adulthood, but emotionally, I was unraveling. Mom and Dennis tried to guide me toward help and even convinced me to attend an AA meeting. But when I mistakenly ended up at a women's meeting, I left thinking, "Why would I ever bother again?" My denial was thick enough to deflect any suggestion that I truly needed help.

That summer after freshman year, I discovered just how threatening sober living felt. No keg parties, no cocaine, no boisterous fraternity atmosphere to drown out my insecurities. Alone with my thoughts and the Alaskan skyline, fear crept in—the fear of my father, fear of quiet, fear of the chaos in my own mind. Drinking had become my way of burying these anxieties. The moment I was back among the Dartmouth crowd, campus life's comforting illusions erased my guilt, and I drank harder than ever, desperate to convince myself everything was normal.

Betrayals and Crossed Boundaries

My illusions about partying "harmlessly" didn't last. The more I drank, the more lines of human decency I crossed. Even as I advanced into sophomore and junior years, my behavior around women and relationships became a dark pattern of bragging, pushing boundaries, and oblivious cruelty.

At the fraternity house, we entertained ourselves by outdoing each other in hooking up with girls—casually, carelessly. I didn't think about consequences until one shocking example of my own callousness forced me to see what I was doing. One morning, I woke to a friend confronting me: a girl was incensed because I had drunkenly barged into her room, demanding sex the night before. I remembered nothing. "I'm sorry," I told her, feeling empty. Her exasperated remark—"If you'd just asked me like a human being, it might have been different"—shredded my illusions further. I couldn't even remember if I had forced her. A wave of shame overwhelmed me. But instead of reflecting, I drowned that shame in the next round of drinks.

A similar pattern occurred when I slept with a "nice" sorority student, only to broadcast intimate details of our encounter around campus the next day. It was the same show-off routine I'd used repeatedly to fit in. For me, it was a drunken fling; for her, it destroyed her senior year. Fraternity guys began making crass jokes, harassing, and objectifying her—all because of my reckless talk. Years later, when I ran into her, I truly understood the weight of the damage I had done. She spelled out clearly the scorn, unwanted attention, and gossip she endured. I felt gutted, recognizing that the humiliation she experienced was entirely my doing.

Another betrayal unfolded when I seduced the girlfriend of my own fraternity “Little Bro”—a young woman who admired me deeply. She became pregnant and tearfully asked me for help covering the cost of an abortion and requested my company at the clinic. I gave her half the money but got drunk on the day she needed me, leaving her to face the procedure alone. She rightfully rebuked me in a letter months afterward. My illusions of harmless partying shattered once again.

These stories might sound like cautionary tales from a cruel fraternity movie, except there was no comedic relief. Instead, it was heartbreak, betrayal, and self-loathing—all fueled by my unstoppable alcohol consumption, my broken moral compass, and fear-driven attempts to impress others. Yet each time, I lied to myself, believing the next party or next line would somehow erase the shame.

Academic Decay and Survival

Meanwhile, academically, I continued sliding. I'd enroll in "gut classes" like Bio 2 (nicknamed "Human Reproduction" or "Rocks-Off for Jocks"), expecting an easy B, only to discover that professors tested purely on lectures I never attended. I bombed midterms, saved only by generous grading curves.

Another time, I took an English class thinking I'd easily breeze through because the assignments were essays. My overconfidence backfired badly. I turned in sloppy papers, failing the first two assignments. Barely rebounding with an outlandish topic on the third paper, I scraped by with a C overall. Doing the bare minimum became my standard. My drinking consumed vast amounts of time—time to get wasted, time to recover, time to repeat the cycle. Yet Dartmouth's coursework was far from trivial. Each semester, I skated along, barely hanging by a thread, crafting half-hearted papers that showed occasional glimpses of brilliance overshadowed by savage hangovers.

Gone was the high school star who amazed teachers. More days than not, I missed classes, sleeping off blackouts. Professors occasionally sent messages: "We'd like to actually see the student behind these papers." I almost never appeared.

Despite the downward spiral, I maintained enough cunning and memory to pass final exams or piece together final projects. Within the fractured fraternity culture, missing classes and living for the next party felt normal. I convinced myself: Once you graduate, none of this will matter. You'll straighten out then. But that was just another lie. Each year, my tether to normal functioning grew thinner, and visits back to Alaska forced me to confront my father's haunting presence—an undercurrent of terror that drove me right back to the bottle.

Another Run-In with Sam

As senior year approached, my mother informed me I'd have to come home for a stint, and I dreaded the possibility of encountering Sam. The memory of him spontaneously confronting me on an Anchorage street corner still left me shaking. I'd turned around to see him a few feet away—my 5'11", 225-pound father who carried an arsenal of old resentments. In an instant, raw panic exploded inside me. Without thinking, I bolted, sprinting until my lungs burned. That flight response told me everything: I was still the little boy who feared his father's belt, fists, or worse. All the frat bravado on campus couldn't stand up to Sam's shadow. I realized that, while I pretended to be some fearless rager, I was petrified at my core.

Eventually, I made it back to Dartmouth for the final push. My illusions that this life was workable hit a final snag. In the scramble to graduate, I realized I'd neglected a mandatory summer term. That meant I'd watch my peers graduate in the spring while I still owed a few credits. My mother flew in for the ceremony, only to see me not crossing the stage. It was humiliating. I spent an anticlimactic extra summer on campus, halfheartedly finishing requirements, fueling more nights of lonely drinking in near-empty dorms. My academic illusions lay in shards now. I'd still earn my degree—a history major with middling grades—but the sense of having "gotten away with something" clashed with an inner knowledge: I had barely survived, and I was a wreck.

Harsh Light on the Truth

By the time I officially left Dartmouth in mid-1984, the illusions that had propped me up for four years were in tatters. The idea that partying was harmless, that I was still morally decent, that I could handle my father's specter or the shameful secrets piling up—none could withstand the raw truth. My life was spinning out of control, and the cracks in my spirit had grown into wide fissures. A few friends dared to call me out: "Ken, you ever think you're drinking too much?" or "You good, man? You don't seem like yourself." I brushed them away, conjuring one last story about how college was supposed to be wild, how every frat had "that guy," and I was just fulfilling the role.

Behind the scenes, I was closer to the edge than anyone realized—including myself. The seeds of hardcore addiction had been sown. The pains of my father's abuse, plus the racial tensions and identity crises at Dartmouth, had watered them. Lies, betrayals, and casual cruelty became the noxious fertilizer. Soon enough, those seeds would bloom into something far more destructive once I was out in the real world, free from any remaining structure. Graduation should have symbolized success; instead, it signaled a descent that would land me even deeper in the chaos I was already courting.

Looking back, I realize the illusions—my illusions—were the scaffolding I used to navigate an environment in which I never felt safe. Now that scaffold was splintering at every joint. My next steps, beyond Dartmouth, would reveal just how unchecked my alcoholism and other addictions had become, and how the harsh realities of fatherhood, street life, and addiction would merge into a kind of maelstrom I couldn't have predicted.

CHAPTER 3: MY REFLECTIONS

The cracks often show up before the full collapse; they're the warning signs. Catching them early—choosing to pause, reflect, or seek help—can divert a crisis from becoming catastrophe. It's not easy to pause in the middle of life's parties and pressures, but learning from the splintered illusions might be the difference between breaking free or breaking down.

1. **Beware of "*Harmless*" Habits** – What starts as partying or social drinking can quickly escalate. If you find yourself looking for ways to justify or hide how much you use—or if you regularly wake up with no memory of the night before—take note. Those can be the early signposts of a spiral.
2. **Emotional Debt Always Comes Due** – Suppressing anger, shame, or past trauma doesn't eliminate it; it only strengthens the hold these emotions have. Unaddressed pain is like a hidden sinkhole: you never know which moment will make the ground cave beneath you.
3. **Guilt Versus Amends** – Moments of regret—like hurting someone through gossip or betrayal—carry lessons. If you find yourself reliving those

mistakes, remember it's never too early (or too late) to acknowledge them and try to make amends. Guilt left unresolved can morph into a heavier burden than you realize.

4. **Masks Eventually Crumble** – Putting up illusions —whether it's being "the party guy" or acting like a carefree star student—only works for a time. If you feel your self-worth depends on approval from a social circle, step back and ask yourself which deeper issue you're avoiding.
5. **Face the Fears** – Whether it's an abusive parent or an inner sense of unworthiness, running only prolongs the pain. True relief starts with acknowledging what you're most afraid of and mustering the courage to confront it—through therapy, trusted friends, support groups, or healthy mentors.
6. **Don't Play In The Gray** – Let's say white is good and black is bad. It might be harmless at first. But it's like flirting. You go to a bar to shoot pool you're playing in the gray.

PART TWO
THE DESCENT INTO STREET LIFE

CHAPTER 4
PUSHING MORE BOUNDARIES

By the time 1984 rolled around, most of my Dartmouth peers were celebrating their graduation with champagne toasts and brand-new cars. Me? I was back in Anchorage, sprawled on my mom's couch, deep in a fog of depression, my direction long since derailed. I had no bright future lined up—just a darkness that sapped the life out of me each passing day.

Late one September morning, Mom shook me awake.

"Kenneth," she said softly, "I want to take you somewhere."

Still half-asleep, I shot up, certain my new ride was finally coming—some handshake agreement, I thought, where I'd get my post-Dartmouth present. The illusions got me so hyped I barely noticed the route we were taking. But I definitely noticed when we drove right past the biggest car dealerships in Anchorage, skipping each row of shiny Chevys, Hondas, and Fords. She turned onto Fireweed Lane, stopping outside a modest brick building labeled "North Point Treatment Center."

I stared at that sign, at my mom, then back at the building. No car. No congratulatory pep talk. Instead, I was about to check myself into my first outpatient treatment program for alcoholism—and I was only twenty-one years old. She'd chosen an entirely different "gift" for me. At that moment, I wished the pavement would swallow me whole, but I followed her inside.

Trying On Sobriety–Atheist Style

North Point was a faith-based treatment center, which was tough for me because I was an atheist and had no desire to believe otherwise. I'd never felt any personal connection with God, had never seen any burning bush or parted sea. As far as I was concerned, God left me at birth. So, it wasn't easy to open my heart to their calls for surrender and spiritual help. But in the spirit of going along to get along—and maybe to placate Mom—I stuck around.

I began attending meetings of Alcoholics Anonymous, telling everyone (and myself) that drinking was my only problem, and I'd fix it by quitting. I conveniently left out the fact that I had no intention of stopping weed or cocaine. In my mind, weed was harmless, and cocaine was just something to turn parties up a notch. Alcohol was the culprit, I decided—if I just cut that out, I'd be good as gold.

Of course, I was nowhere near dealing with the bigger truth: I had fallen in love with chemically shifting my perception of reality, no matter the substance. Pain, depression, fear—didn't matter. I wanted a cloud to float on. I was an uncommitted attendee at best—picking whichever AA steps I liked and skimming over the rest. You might call it "the Chinese menu method" of recovery: Step 1 from Column A, Step 4 from Column B, skip Steps 5–9 altogether. Unsurprisingly, that approach rarely ends well.

For a moment, though, it seemed like I was on track. I picked up a job at an office supply store—just enough stable income to keep me from drowning and keep Mom off my back. Each day I put on a halfway decent face, sober from booze but still sneaking hits of weed at home, convinced I'd solved my "real" problem.

Into Modeling and Mixed Messages

One Saturday, I was at a club called Yesterdays, high on some good weed and feeling bulletproof. A DJ buddy told me about a woman roaming the crowd, taking pictures of handsome men for a project. "She's scouting for some new magazine," he said, winking at me. I brushed him off with a laugh—I had no interest in being her next model.

But then she found me—came right up, camera around her neck, pitch on her lips.

"Hey, you mind posing? You've got a look I'd love to feature."

I was too stoned and unimpressed to care. "No thanks," I said. She came back a second time, pushing her luck. I said no again—maybe with a bit more edge, certain her idea was nonsense.

But the third time, I actually looked at her. Really looked. She was gorgeous. Striking eyes, sharp wit, easy confidence. My guard wavered. It's funny how quickly "No way" turns into "Sure, why not?" when seduction is involved. Before the night was over, I'd agreed to take pictures—and to take her home with me.

Something about her intelligence and warmth tugged at me, so I tried a gentlemanly approach. I told her maybe we should just talk, take it slow. Of course, that vow of chastity didn't hold through the night, but I did like her beyond lust. Her name was Janice, and she was behind this new single-men's magazine project called Alaska Single Men. She was sure I'd be perfect for it.

Only problem? I was already juggling a "friends with benefits" arrangement with another woman, Beth. She and I had a no-questions, no-judgment deal. I liked that freedom, and in my messed-up mind, it didn't conflict with wanting something deeper with Janice. I was so sure I could pull it all off.

Double Life, Double Trouble

For a while, I enjoyed the thrill—secret lunches in bed with Beth on my break from work, lavish date nights and a budding romance with Janice whenever our schedules lined up. I assumed I was unstoppable. But soon enough, the ceiling caved in.

Janice confronted me, demanding I come clean. In a rare moment of partial honesty, I confessed I'd slept with Beth. I swore it was over, even though "over" definitely wasn't part of the arrangement Beth and I had. Rather than digging deeper into my self-sabotage, I tried slapping a bandage on it: "I promise, I'll never see her again." If only it were that simple.

Janice tried. She seemed willing to bury the hatchet. But then she made a discovery worse than my confession—she found my personal journal. In it, I'd detailed the entire fiasco: how I balanced my time between the two women, my strategies for skipping out of work to see Beth, and all the justifications I'd used to keep it going.

Getting caught with your lies in plain text is a special kind of ugly. She felt betrayed, and I felt violated that she'd snooped in my private diary. My moral compass was skewed: I'd cheated, yet her invasion of my privacy outraged me. We were swirling in a blender of guilt, anger, heartbreak, and mistrust. It all fell apart. Janice kicked me out of her life.

Ironically, she still followed through on featuring me in Alaska Single Men's very first issue. That magazine became a phenomenon—three or four of us were Black men in a sea of lumberjacks, fishermen, and genuine Alaskan "mountain men." The issue blew up, capturing the imagination of people around the country and making Alaska Single Men a mini pop-culture event before social media existed.

At the same time, I started dabbling more in modeling: runway gigs for local clothing stores, print work, even the occasional TV commercial. I was living a life that looked glamorous from the outside. There were whispers of me being featured on PM Magazine, a national TV show. Then I actually got a call for an interview with Hugh Downs from PM Magazine. Next, I was invited to appear on the rising phenomenon, The Oprah Winfrey Show—my big break, right?

One problem: I'd quietly relapsed on alcohol again. I wasn't sober enough to show up on a bus bench, let alone a nationally televised talk show. The opportunity evaporated, lost to the bottle and the illusions I insisted on preserving.

High-Powered Sales, Low-Commitment Sobriety

Eventually, I left my office supply gig and landed a sales position with the 3M corporation, a recognized name in office products. It felt like another rung up the ladder—my suits got nicer, my watch flashier, and my bank account healthier. At 22, I was pulling in roughly fifty grand a year, the equivalent of well over six figures now. Mom was proud I'd found what she called a "real job." I guess I was proud too. I smelled good, looked good, and in my head, that was enough to gloss over everything else unraveling behind the scenes.

I also doubled down on "proving" I wasn't an alcoholic. I'd rejoined AA, picking up my sobriety chips while secretly making sure I had a joint for afterward. If I felt guilty for skipping anything at a meeting, I'd reframe it: "I'm attending the parts that matter." I'd avoided hard liquor for a bit, so I gave myself gold stars for that. In social settings, I'd grab "near beer" like Kaliber or Clausthaler—convincing everyone (and maybe myself) that I was participating responsibly and harmlessly. Meanwhile, the "real" me was snorting coke, smoking weed, and partying to oblivion on weekends. Alcohol might have been the gateway, but my other vices were still pushing me toward the same deep end.

Party Ken was the life of the happy-hour crew. My suits were pressed, my lines slick, and if you wanted a good time, you invited me. Did it matter that I was floating on substances to keep my mood up? Not if you asked me back then. I measured my success by the size of my paycheck and the number of compliments on my tie. The rest was just details.

Amid all this, quiet dread was building. I could feel my illusions wearing thin. Relapse was a vague whisper in the corner of my mind, but I kept dancing around it, certain I was fully in control.

I had no idea how quickly that illusion would splinter. This easy, confident salesman persona would soon slip from my grasp. The list of missed opportunities was growing longer—Oprah, modeling deals, relationships disintegrating in slow motion. I might have still been in denial, but the cracks in my façade were becoming harder to ignore.

Pushing the Boundaries

Looking back, those months before I dove into the Seattle apartment scene were a volatile mix of ambition, recklessness, and denial. I see it now as a time of trying to outrun my reality. I was stacking illusions: illusions I could hide a double life, illusions I wasn't a "real" alcoholic if I skipped vodka and stuck to near beers, illusions my heartbreaks and betrayals could be patched over with quick fixes and half-apologies.

But illusions can only stretch so far. Eventually, something hits them—whether it's a breakup, a missed flight, or an unexpected chance at national TV—and the entire mirage cracks. I was about to discover that the adrenaline from fast-living, fast-talking hustle always comes with a price tag.

Below all that bravado, I was still the depressed Dartmouth kid who once slept for days on his mother's couch. No matter how many suits I bought or near beers I sipped, the pain was still there, waiting. And with every new substance I allowed into my routine—weed, cocaine, or "just a little wine" —I was feeding that addictive monster a bigger appetite for destruction. Illusions always have their limits, and I was about to slam straight into mine.

CHAPTER 4: MY REFLECTIONS

Looking back on this stretch of life, I see how I kept testing the limits—whether it was half-hearted recovery, cheating in relationships, or dabbling in new substances. Every boundary I crossed fed my denial: "I'm only skipping the parts of AA I don't like," or "I'm only using weed, so I must be fine," or "I can juggle two girlfriends without anyone getting hurt." The reality? Each move tightened addiction's grip on me and left me less able to handle real life.

1. **Glamour Can Be a Mirage** - A magazine shoot or a potential spot on Oprah doesn't guarantee peace. You can be "successful" on the outside yet tormented inside. Real stability starts with inner work, not external attention.
2. **Selective Sobriety Doesn't Work** - I convinced myself I'd beaten alcohol by switching to near beer, ignoring that I was still relying on weed and coke. If the core obsession remains, swapping substances is just a different road to the same dark place.
3. **Double Lives Breed Double Chaos** - Trying to balance two relationships or half-in/half-out of recovery multiplies secrets and lies. Eventually, it

all collapses, often in the most humiliating or painful ways.

4. **Facing Fear—But Missing the Healing** - Standing up to my father freed me from one specific terror, but it didn't address my emotional damage. Real healing demands more than confronting a person; it requires confronting yourself.
5. **The Lure of Denial** - Each relapse or missed opportunity (like the Hawaii trip fiasco) was a clear warning sign. Yet I brushed it off with "It's not that bad." Denial let me keep stumbling until the consequences stacked too high to ignore.

CHAPTER 5
CRACKS TURNED TO CANYONS

Somewhere between my earnest attempts at staying sober and my ongoing fling with weed and cocaine, I decided it was time to move out of my mom's house. I'd love to say I left because I felt confident, ready to handle real independence. But deep down, it was more about my restless craving for bigger highs and zero accountability. My new roommate turned out to be the kind of person every budding addict warns you about—but never believes they'll become.

A White Flame of Freebase

When he introduced me to freebase cocaine, it was like a whole new Pandora's box got flung open. He explained the chemistry of it with a half-serious grin: freeing the base from cocaine hydrochloride using ether or ammonia—stuff that could blow your face off if you weren't careful. I'd never heard such a crash course in chemistry outside a lab. But the selling point? It hit fast, like lightning striking your brain.

I tried it maybe two or three times. The immediate rush was all-consuming, every nerve ablaze. And then—like the flick of a cruel switch—my body and mind sank into a depression so dense I thought the weight might crush me. It was as if every good feeling got borrowed from the future, then the debt collector showed up with interest. I remember telling myself, "Never again," figuring I could escape this particular hell by sheer willpower.

And, strangely enough, I did stop freebasing that month, fully convinced I'd dodged a bullet. It didn't matter that I still had a love affair with snorting regular cocaine and smoking weed all day; I bragged that I never "really" got into freebase, so I must be in control. That's the kind of logic an addict uses to pat themselves on the back.

A Two-Year Mirage

Somehow, I remained sober from alcohol for two years. Alcohol was always my main demon, but here I was, feeding my other vices—weed, powder cocaine, casual sex—while smugly calling myself "sober." My job at the time was decent, my daily routine fairly stable if you didn't peer too closely. But beneath that surface was a thick layer of self-pity morphing from the raw depression I carried.

To the outside world, I looked okay. Inside, the cracks were widening. Maybe that's why I got it in my head to settle some old business—namely, the fear of Sam. If there was a glimmer of me wanting genuine progress in life, it came in the form of confronting my father.

I'd been coasting along—smoking weed, doing a little powder cocaine, convinced I was managing the fallout of life—yet I knew there was an itch I had to scratch. I had to confront Sam if I ever hoped to stop seeing him in my nightmares. The fear gnawed at me; a lingering aftertaste of all those years when he was the giant in the shadows. So, I asked my older brother Michael to come with me to see our father. Michael was Sam's son from a previous marriage, ten years older, and never seemed afraid of him. If I was going to stand at Sam's door, I needed that kind of confidence at my side.

He lived in this place called Kings Row off 15th Street—a run-down apartment complex that smelled of mildew, stale liquor, and regret. The place matched what I pictured Sam's life had become. As we walked up to his door, each step weighed a hundred pounds. I could feel my pulse in my ears, so loud I thought Michael might hear it.

When I reached out to press the buzzer, I froze. Literally froze. In that split second, I was a kid again—feeling the belt, the chainsaw, the icy stare, the endless threats. Every survival instinct screamed at me to turn around and leave. Michael put a hand on my shoulder and said quietly, "It's alright, Ken. I'm right here."

I don't know how, but that nudged me forward. I rang the bell, half-expecting Sam to tear the door off its hinges. Instead, he opened it slowly, and what I saw nearly shook me more than if he'd swung at me: he looked small. Time and booze had shriveled him into a shell of the raging man I'd feared. This wasn't the unstoppable monster from my nightmares; this was a sad, tired old drunk.

We stepped inside, wary but determined. It was cramped—an old chair, a table scattered with empty bottles. The air felt stale, weighed down by regrets. For a moment, we just stood there, sizing each other up like strangers. Then we managed a conversation—Michael and I on the sagging couch, Sam in his chair, slumped over, talking about how life had gotten away from him. It was surreal. He barely looked me in the eye. I felt pity, maybe even anger at how pathetic he'd become. But more than that, I realized something life-changing: He can't hurt me anymore. The man who once filled my world with terror was powerless now.

I walked out that day with a sense of finality. I wasn't sure if I forgave Sam, but I did stop fearing him. The switch flipped off—that eternal "What if he kills me?" loop in my head. You'd think that'd be the end of the story—closure. But Sam's ghost had one more chapter up its sleeve.

A Familiar Cocktail of Violence

Michael and I started dropping by more often, making sure Sam wasn't dead in his apartment. One Saturday morning, we visited him at his apartment—set just above ground level—and saw he was in bad shape. He was hungover, eyes bloodshot, reeking of stale brandy. A small automatic handgun lay on the table in front of him, like a silent dare.

He glanced at it, then at us, and mumbled, "I'm just tired of living." For a second, it felt twistedly ironic; all my life, I'd daydreamed about a reality where he no longer existed. Now he was the one ready to check out. We tried to take the gun, but he insisted the bullets weren't even in it—he only kept it for burglars in that sketchy neighborhood. Eventually, we left him there, gun at his elbow, feeling uneasy but unsure what else to do.

The next day was Sunday, so I went to visit my mom's condo in Bootleggers Cove. She and Dennis—a tough corrections officer who wasn't scared of Sam or any man—were cooking dinner. Through the window, I spotted Sam in his car, obviously drunk, but by now it was routine: Mom would call the police, Sam would vanish. We ate dinner as if nothing unusual had happened.

Not twenty-four hours later, I got a call at work from Roxie, my mother's secretary: "Kenneth, Kenneth! Sam's shot Irene!" Her voice was frayed, hysterical. She told me Mom was at Providence Hospital. Despite the intensity of her words, I recall feeling...blank. Like I'd hit some inner breaker switch. A numb voice in my head just said, Of course he did.

I told my boss, Bobby, "Hey, my mom's been shot—can I take a little time off?" He stared at me like I'd just announced aliens landed in the parking lot, and I shrugged it off. I arrived at the hospital to see Mom on a gurney, blood seeping everywhere. There was a flicker of relief in her eyes that I was alive, because Sam had apparently planned to shoot me, too. He'd burst into her office area, ignoring the restraining order, drunk as ever, demanding to see her. Her secretaries panicked, but she said, "Let him come down the hall to my office. I'll handle it."

When she told him calmly, "Sam, you can't be here," he pulled out a .25 automatic and shot her in the leg. She collapsed, and he kept firing—five more rounds, four hitting her point-blank. While he did it, he declared his intention to kill me next, making it crystal clear she was about to die, and I wasn't far behind. Miraculously, the gun jammed before he emptied the entire clip. Then he left her there and went home to pass out.

Watching her lying there, moments from surgery, I felt no emotional shock—just a mechanical sense that this was a situation that needed managing. I asked if she needed anything, and she said, "Yes, my purse." I grabbed it, and I... left. I clocked back in at work, not finding out until the end of the day whether or not she was even alive post-surgery. That was the depth of my dissociation.

Sam was arrested in his apartment, still drunk. And me? I just carried on—like usual. The reality that he'd nearly killed her (and wanted me dead too) felt as if it happened in a TV show. Sometimes I think the scariest part wasn't what Sam did; it was how unshaken I was by it.

In a way, facing him at Kings Row freed me from the cringing terror I'd grown up with. But the aftermath—a bullet-ridden mother, a father hauled off in handcuffs, and my eerie calm—showed how deeply broken I was inside. Years of brutality had taught me survival, but it also robbed me of normal human reactions like horror or despair. If Sam was a loaded gun, I was an empty vessel, drained of feeling. And in that hollow state, I'd soon find my addictions spiraling into a whole new territory of chaos, shaped by the same numbness that once let me walk away from my bleeding mother.

Cracks Becoming Canyons

By August 1986, I was somehow holding life together—though "together" was a fragile term. That's when I took a trip to Hawaii, feeling like I deserved some slice of paradise. I'd been off booze for two years. Why not celebrate?

Someone handed me a Blue Hawaiian—rum, pineapple juice, sweet-and-sour mix, Blue Curaçao. Nothing fancy, but it looked cheerful enough. One won't kill me, I thought. After all, I wasn't a real alcoholic anymore, right?

Within forty-eight hours, I was broke. Couldn't even pay for my return ticket. I had to beg my mom to wire me money so I could limp back to Alaska. Once again, my entire flimsy structure collapsed the moment alcohol seeped in. The weed and powder cocaine? Manageable, I told myself. But booze tore me up every time—and I kept letting it in. I'd lose jobs, cheat on partners, or wake up in random hotel rooms. By this point, I was so used to burning bridges that I could barely feel the sting of betrayal anymore.

But the next year would prove even more precarious. Mom, now recovering from her injuries, was moving to Washington. My big brain concluded that a "geographical cure" might solve everything. If I went somewhere new, somewhere nobody knew me, maybe I could reinvent how I drank, used, and lived. Spoiler alert: that never works. But in 1988, I was too desperate—and too foolish—to see it any other way.

A New Frontier of Old Habits

My first night in Seattle, I strolled into this bar called 611 near Pioneer Square. One drink turned into five, which turned into who-knows-how-many. Day two, I explored the city's nightlife: Harry's Backroom, Brass Connection, Neighbors. I was a star in my own rock opera, dancing on bar tops in my mind.

I found a legitimate job in Spokane, selling microfilm machines to rural banks in Montana, Idaho, and eastern Washington—places where seeing a sharp-dressed Black man in a bow tie caused bigger stares than I'd ever known. So I'd suit up in my Hickey Freeman suits and Allen Edmonds shoes and stride into these small-town offices, trying to sell them on advanced document storage. But my biggest sale was always the façade that I was smooth, thriving, and definitely *not* an alcoholic.

The truth? I carried the same self-destructive patterns from Anchorage. I'd go out after work, drink until I could barely see, and expect different outcomes. My illusions of control stayed afloat until one night I left a club in downtown Spokane, hammered out of my mind, and crashed my company car. I was so out of it that I abandoned the car, walked home, and passed out. The cops banged on my door the next morning, asking why my sedan was still in the middle of the street. I couldn't recall a damn thing.

And that was it—the job was gone, any dignity I had left drained. Opening my fridge, I saw only mustard and two hot dog buns. I sat there, munching stale bread slathered with cheap mustard, feeling like the biggest failure in the world. *Dartmouth degree, my ass.*

I spiraled fast. After all the breaks—modeled in a magazine, had a good job, mother's unconditional love—here I was, this Ivy League graduate scarfing mustard buns in a near-empty apartment, jobless, alone, and once again flirting with the idea that life might not be worth continuing.

Bridge Over the Edge

The next morning, I wandered to the Spokane Falls Bridge, staring at the turbulent waters and jagged rocks below. I pictured myself ending it, letting the water swallow me whole. A thousand cuts from my failures, betrayals, and that haunting self-talk that I wasn't wanted—any of it was enough to make me leap.

But I had one last thread of hope: I called Mom collect, ready to say goodbye if she didn't pick up. She answered on the first ring. Somehow, she'd sensed my desperation before the words came out. She told me she'd already arranged a spot at Sundown M Ranch, an inpatient facility in Yakima. It was as if she'd never doubted for a second that I would come to this place, needing rescue.

Twenty-four hours later, I was on a bus with only the clothes on my back, heading to a twenty-eight-day "spin dry." Sundown M Ranch was not a party spa. It was a real-deal treatment center. But for someone as far gone as me, twenty-eight days was just a drop in the ocean. Still, it was another shot at sobriety—a forced pause button on the chaos.

Seattle's Second Chance

After I got out, I moved to Seattle proper, where my uncle, Reverend McKinney—pastor of Mount Zion Baptist Church —provided me with a three-bedroom apartment for a measly three hundred bucks a month. It was practically a dream scenario: a stable home right by the church, with the shadow of family support across the street. I enrolled in outpatient counseling at Therapeutic Health Services (THS) with Reverend Steve Johnson, who genuinely seemed determined to keep me on the rails.

I scored a job at Nordstrom, which was *perfect* for the polished, image-conscious me I liked to flaunt. Between the therapy sessions and the crisp dress shirts, I felt buoyed by new optimism. *This time,* I swore, I'd keep it together. I felt like I'd found a little equilibrium.

But that old, ominous pattern soon slithered back in. I started missing therapy sessions. One innocent drink led to two, which led to stumbling home at 21st and Madison, hammered. My illusions about having conquered alcohol again unraveled. And with each unraveling, the "high" I was forever chasing dragged me a step closer to places darker than I'd imagined—straight toward the streets.

CHAPTER 5: MY REFLECTIONS

I called this period "Lost in the High" for a reason: every time I tasted a new rush—crack, freebase, booze after a sober streak—it felt like stepping into a dream world. But once the rush wore off, I'd crash even lower than before. My father nearly killing my mother should have jolted me, but I'd grown so numb that I filed the trauma away without dealing with it. Instead, I chased dopamine hits to dodge pain. In reality, I was setting myself up for the streets.

1. **Trauma Numbs Before It Heals** - Seeing my mom shot, confronting Sam—these should have invoked horror. Instead, I shut down. Unprocessed trauma doesn't vanish; it festers, fueling ever-riskier behaviors.
2. **Temporary Victories Can Fool You** - "Two years off alcohol" sounded great, but I replaced drinking with other highs. If the pain or mindset isn't addressed, any so-called "clean time" can be a ticking bomb waiting to detonate.
3. **Geographical Cures Never Solve Inner Wounds** - Moving from Anchorage to Spokane to Seattle, I kept hoping a new city would change my life. But I

carried the same addictive patterns wherever I went. Only an internal shift breaks that cycle.

4. **Confrontation Isn't Completion** - Meeting Sam in that run-down apartment forced me to see him as human, which helped dissolve my terror. But it didn't dissolve my own dysfunctions. Courage in one area doesn't automatically fix everything else.
5. **Denial Is a High in Itself** - I kept telling myself, "I'll handle it," or "It's just one drink." That mindset is as addictive as any substance because it shields you from reality. True change starts with busting through denial.

CHAPTER 6
KNOW WHERE TO GO

At the intersection of Madison Street and 19th—now reverently named Rev. Dr. S. McKinney Ave—stands Mount Zion Baptist Church, a place of refuge for many. For me, it came with a three-bedroom apartment that was supposed to be my fresh start, a haven where I might finally achieve sobriety. After all, proximity to holiness should help, right? Unfortunately, my counselor, Rev. Johnson, didn't know I was still obsessed with that "payday promise": I'd stop at the bar for just one or two beers after work—somehow forgetting I was an alcoholic. My ritual was predictable: polished shoes, optimistic grin, a cheerful "I'm only staying thirty minutes." Then, eight or ten beers later, I'd stagger home, cursing myself but never stopping.

The Lure of a New Room

In outpatient treatment at THS, I met all kinds of folks, and one I clicked with was Matthew—a gay Black guy from Los

Angeles who had a knack for seeing through my BS. He was the same age as me, equally deep in his own struggles, but we bonded over our shared desire to be better than our demons. When Rev. Johnson asked if I'd mind having some new roommates in my three-bedroom apartment—two guys also in the program—I figured, Sure, why not? A bit more rent money, a little company. Only, I should've known that more bodies meant more chaos if one of them was chasing the same high I couldn't resist.

They arrived shortly after, their two rooms barely furnished. One night, I came home and found them chatting excitedly in the living room—only to watch them vanish into a room together, emerging a while later looking sullen. My curiosity piqued, I asked, "What's up?" That's when they offered me my first rock of crack cocaine. For all my misadventures, I'd never seen crack in person. Sure, I'd freebased once or twice in the past, but freebase was a more delicate, ammonia-and-ether madness. Crack, on the other hand, was touted as easy, cheap, and oh-so-intense.

One of them shoved a tiny rock into my hand and explained: "You put this on a little piece of Brillo in a glass tube—called a straight shooter—melt it with a lighter, and inhale." Seemed simple enough. He rattled off details about burning off the copper coating on the Brillo, how the crystals formed on the glass, and how pushing the pipe every so often gave you an extra concentrated rush. They kept talking chemistry, but my mind buzzed at the thought of a new high.

At first, I didn't feel anything—and, like a true addict, I refused to accept defeat. If the initial hits didn't work, I'd try more, or hold the flame a second longer, or get a better angle. Eventually, I inhaled the smoke, and bam: My head swam, bells literally ringing in my ears. We call that a "bell ringer"—the white-hot tingle that screams, *You're beyond high now*. It took me two minutes to become hooked, if that. Alcohol had seduced me slowly back in college; crack was a high-speed train that wouldn't wait for me to decide.

My Truth Was Brutal

I was already an alcoholic masking with weed and powder coke. Now, I'd added another lethal item to the menu. A single bell ringer was all it took to send me barreling into a new dimension of dependency. And if there's one thing crack demands, it's more—always more. Unlike drinking, which could last for hours, the crack high peaked fast and crashed just as quickly, leaving me depressed, restless, and desperate to chase that fleeting jolt again. It also dumped paranoia into the mix. Even if I stood on a deserted street at noon, I'd be sure a squad of undercover cops or a stick-up crew was lurking in shadows only I could see.

Eating became irrelevant. If my body screamed hunger, my mind shrugged: *We've got crack for that*. In a single binge, I could go days with no real food or water. I'd all but forgotten my initial vow to keep things "controlled." And it took no time for Rev. Johnson to notice something was off with my new roommates—he had them removed from the program's housing. Problem is, I was still there, still craving the next rock.

Converting to a Crack House

With those roommates gone, another slid in—just as cunning, just as deep in the drug world. He pitched a business idea: sell crack. It made perfect sense to my warped logic: I was a salesman by trade, rocking suits at Nordstrom. Why not channel that savvy into something that brought instant profit? A "hinge moment," as I call it—where you swing a door one way or the other, not knowing it's an entrance to disaster.

Turning my church-sponsored apartment into a mini crack den was scandalously easy. We had a system: people climbed the stairs, waited in my living room, I fetched the product from my new roommate's stash, then they either smoked in our living room or paid extra to use a spare bedroom. Walking home from Nordstrom, I'd discover total strangers loitering in every corner of my place, piping away like they owned it. Some nights, a random occupant would poke his head out to wave me off if I accidentally tried to enter my own bedroom. If that wasn't a sign of how fast this mania had exploded, I don't know what was.

One night, I saw something I could never have predicted: a guy showed up cradling a baby—barely older than a newborn. After handing me a "Hey, watch this for me," he disappeared to "grab money." The child just lay there on my living-room floor. I remember thinking, *I don't know the first damn thing about babies.* And I left him squirming while I got high. A couple hours later, the poor kid screamed bloody murder. The father finally returned—but not alone. A cop car trailed behind him. In the swirl of confusion, I explained to the officers the baby wasn't mine, no clue where the dad went. Paranoia shot up, but they let it drop. I turned around and marched back upstairs to keep smoking. That was how numb I'd gotten.

Too High to Sell

Any illusions that dealing would be lucrative crashed into one fatal flaw: I was addicted to my own product. The best buyer was me. At Nordstrom, I was supposed to greet customers with a polished grin, but soon my eyes were bloodshot, my nerves fried. My manager, noticing my performance was as ragged as my nicotine-stained fingertips, fired me.

Losing Nordstrom hammered another nail in the coffin of my illusions. Meanwhile, the apartment descended into chaos—an unregulated flophouse, spiraling beyond my control. In desperation, I called Skip, an old friend from Anchorage who now lived in Seattle. He agreed to rescue me, saying, "Grab your stuff. I'll be outside." I sprinted into my roommate's bedroom—where he lay naked with some girl—stole a wad of cash off his dresser, then bolted. He immediately gave chase, but once we reached the street, Skip waved his pistol, and the chase ended.

I hopped into the car and never looked back.

When Beer and a Gun Become a Plan

Temporarily, I crashed at Skip's place down in Kent, trying to find some foothold. But I was still drinking day after day until my bank account ran dry and my craving for crack roared again. That's when I hatched the dumbest scheme imaginable: a Texaco station sat just a few blocks away, and Skip had a starter pistol in his apartment—a harmless blank gun. But it looked real.

In a drunken fog, I grabbed it, stumbled into the Texaco around midnight, and pointed it at the terrified attendant. "Give me all your change!" I roared. Not the bills, not the safe—just coins. Because that's how brilliant I was. The poor guy emptied the register's coins, and I walked—*yes, walked*—the two and a half blocks back, pockets crammed with quarters and dimes.

The next morning, Skip saw me sprawled on his couch surrounded by random piles of coins, the fake gun lying on the floor. Putting two and two together, he was furious. He beat me good—less than Sam would have, but enough to teach me a humiliating lesson. Then he booted me out, cursing that I'd pulled such a brazen stunt under his roof.

So there I was: a Dartmouth grad, bruised from a friend's fists, with nowhere to stay. Every bridge burned. Out of options. Homeless—for real.

CHAPTER 6: MY REFLECTIONS

In life, there is always a choice—even if it's painful. Sometimes that choice is a late-night collect call to Mom, or a last-ditch phone call to a friend who can rescue you for a night. But if I'm not willing to go someplace better mentally, spiritually, or physically, I'll always default to the dark corners of my addiction. And as I walked away from Skip's place—no money, bruised ribs, and no illusions left—I realized I had nowhere good to go. I was standing on the brink, fully consumed by a life I once swore I'd never touch.

1. **Boundaries Break Down Fast** - Living next to a church meant nothing if I wasn't willing to stop using. Morals or good intentions crumble quickly when addiction takes the driver's seat.
2. **Selling Destruction** - Believing I could sell crack without smoking it was a fantasy. Intelligence doesn't guarantee wisdom. When you're addicted, your "product" becomes your master.
3. **Homelessness Is a Slippery Slope** - After I burned every bridge—friends, jobs, family trust—I found myself literally on the street. That bottomless spiral can feel inevitable once addiction takes full control.

4. **Desperation Fuels Reckless Acts** - My coin-heist from the Texaco shows how irrational I'd become. Under addiction, logic and reason give way to desperation, leading to crimes that risk freedom—and life itself.
5. **It's Not Just Geography, It's Mindset** - I fled apartments, jobs, and even entire states, but I never fled my addiction. You have to change your mind and your heart—otherwise, the next move is just another scene in the same tragic story.

PART THREE
DARK NIGHTS OF THE SOUL

CHAPTER 7
IN AND OUT OF MISSIONS & MOTELS

It was the summer of 1989. I was a homeless alcoholic battling drug addiction. Since leaving Kent, I had somehow found my way to Port Townsend, a bohemian enclave nestled on the Olympic Peninsula northwest of Seattle. My mother lived there, and though I had nowhere else to go, being close to her offered some solace.

With assistance from the county, I received food stamps and a motel voucher—just enough to get me off the streets temporarily. But most of my days were spent drowning in self-pity, washing it down with beer. Crack was out of my reach; I couldn't afford it, nor could I seem to find any. The nights grew cooler, edging toward chilly, and once my motel stay expired, I was back on the streets. I lasted just four days before boarding the next bus to Seattle.

Upon arriving, I went straight to the Seattle Union Gospel Mission (UGM) on 2nd Avenue, marking the beginning of what would become a two-to-three-year cycle of mission hopping. Seattle's missions operated on an unspoken hierarchy, ranked by the quality of services and the company one would keep. At the top was the Salvation Army, followed by Union Gospel Mission, Peniel Mission, Bread of Life Mission, and at the bottom, the Downtown Emergency Shelter Corporation (DESC).

Although I frequented Union Gospel the most, the Salvation Army stood apart as the premier mission. Their long-term programs required work—whether in their modern facility (which, remarkably, housed a two-lane bowling alley), their warehouse sorting clothes (what we called "the rag business"), or their thrift store. In exchange, they offered excellent food and accommodations. But there was a catch: participation demanded physical presence and strict adherence to church attendance. Their structure severely curtailed—or outright eliminated—my ability to return to the streets.

After thirty days, I could earn a pass but had to return for a breathalyzer test. Progression in their system came through commitment: those who demonstrated dedication to the program gradually earned more freedom. For the first time in years, I was in an environment where structure, rather than survival, dictated my choices.

Surviving the Mission System

The missions provided vital services and support to individuals experiencing homelessness or facing other challenges. Throughout my journey, I relied on missions in four different states—Washington, Nevada, California, and Mississippi. Regardless of location, they all operated similarly.

Each mission had a Day Room, a space where the homeless could seek refuge from the weather or simply escape the streets. While these shelters didn't allow sleeping, many would still take the opportunity to rest, heads down on tables, recovering from the exhaustion of street life. Though most missions served multiple meals a day, dinner was typically reserved for residents—those who had agreed to abide by the rules of the house.

Many mission programs were long-term, lasting one to two years, with some individuals staying even longer, working their way up to paid employment. Men and women were separated, and in some cases, people were grouped based on their stage of life. Sobriety was easier to maintain when surrounded by others on the same path. Since most missions were Christian-based, staying often meant exchanging work for shelter. Their ultimate goal was to assist individuals until they were ready to transition into halfway houses or other forms of stable housing.

Entering a mission was a straightforward process: I'd walk in and ask if they had space. If available, they would assign me a bed—sometimes a bunk—or, more commonly, what we called a mat.

I became an expert on mats. Nearly all missions used vinyl mats designed for easy cleaning, as bodily fluids often seeped from those sleeping on them. These mats were foldable, which caused the vinyl to crack, allowing a grim mixture of human fluids and cleaning chemicals to accumulate in the crevices. The smell was always a toss-up—some days the disinfectant won, other days it didn't. For some reason, most mats were green, as if there had been a clearance sale on green vinyl. Some missions took better care of their mats, offering ones with extra padding, but in the end, they were all the same: temporary, stackable, and a means to an end.

At night, we'd be assigned a mat area and sleep until the lights flicked on at 6:30 or 7:00 AM. Then came the morning routine—get up, gather whatever belongings we had, and step back out onto the streets. The cycle repeated itself day after day, until something—anything—interrupted it.

For those who still cared about me, knowing I was in a shelter at least meant I was alive and reachable. One day, I received a message: Contact Aunt Pauline.

When I called her, she said, "Kenneth, you need to go to Port Townsend. Irene tried to commit suicide."

Aunt Pauline bought me a bus ticket, and I traveled to see my mother in the hospital. By then, I was so deep into my addiction that my reaction was...nothing. Apathy. My emotions had drained dry long ago, leaving a hollow space where feeling used to exist. I stood there, numb, yet somewhere beneath that emptiness, I was relieved she had survived.

She needed rest, and I needed an escape. When I got to her home, my body ached for a fix. I went straight to her bedroom, opened the medicine cabinet, and found the only bottle of pills there. I crushed them, melted them down, and injected them.

I didn't feel much.

Desperation, Deals, and the Downward Spiral

My mother survived her suicide attempt, but she hadn't yet recovered from the shooting. Two bullets remained lodged in her body, constant reminders of the violence she had endured. Mentally, emotionally, and physically, she was shattered. Spiritually, she felt abandoned. She questioned herself as a mother, wondering where she had gone wrong and what she could have done differently to change my course in life.

Her relationship with Dennis was crumbling. He had disappeared, leaving her alone—just as alone as I had been with my own demons. My mother had always valued her role as a loved and cherished woman, yet here she was: a current husband likely having an affair, a former husband who had tried to kill her, and an only child—me, Kenneth John Miller—who hadn't even shed a tear when he saw her bleeding out on a hospital gurney, five bullet holes tearing through her body.

It was too much. The pain—the loneliness—became unbearable. She wanted it to stop. The thought that haunted her most was simple yet devastating: "Ken doesn't love me." She swallowed a bottle of sleeping pills and lay down for what she intended to be her final rest. But it wasn't her time.

To this day, she could never recall how she ended up at the hospital or how Aunt Pauline learned about her suicide attempt. It was as if some unseen force had intervened. Regardless of how she got there, she was alive. And once I saw she was in good hands, I returned to the streets.

Still seeking an escape—from my pain, my past, myself—I

returned to Seattle and went to Neighbours, a bar off Broadway. I drank until a man approached me. We talked, and then he made me an offer: if I engaged in sexual acts with him, he would provide for me financially and give me a place to stay. I had been propositioned.

Most people think prostitution is simply the exchange of money for sex. I don't see it that way. Prostitution is the exchange of self in return for whatever it is you're seeking. I went home with him, and we had sex. Or rather, he had sex with my body—my mind was elsewhere.

The next morning, I felt nothing but disgust. Shame clung to me like filth I couldn't wash off. I had sold myself for a warm bed, for security, for the promise of something resembling stability. I told myself it wasn't the first time I had been with a man. At least this time, it was my choice, made with a relatively sound mind. Then, something unexpected: relief.

I had a place to sleep, a place to shower. That man became my first sugar daddy. I was now officially a male prostitute. Ironically, if he had handed me a ring instead of cash, society would have simply called me his partner. Eventually, I left him and moved to Lynnwood, Washington, where I found a job at a construction firm. I rented a mother-in-law suite inside someone's house. I even bought a car for $300. For the first time in a long time, it felt like I was rebuilding my life.

Then I had two beers. That was all it took before I started searching for crack. My quartet of self-destruction—self-pity, arrogance, alcohol, and cocaine—once again found its harmony, and before long, I was broke. Again.

I had a bank account, but keeping money in it was

another story. I found a way around that. At grocery stores, I began writing bad checks—buying a few dollars' worth of food and alcohol while getting $40 cash back. That was enough for a few rocks. Once I was high, I didn't even need the food anymore. The store's cash became my drug fund. It wasn't a perfect system, but it worked—for a while. As long as I balanced my checks correctly, I had found a loophole for a perpetual supply. All I had to do was consume responsibly. After writing a few checks, I had enough cash to hit a bar. I drank freely, confident in my scheme. When I was done, I got into my $300 car and headed home.

I don't know if I swerved, missed a stoplight, or forgot to use my blinker, but none of that mattered when I saw the flashing red and blue lights in my rearview mirror. I had been drinking. I had been driving. And I had been caught.

The field sobriety test was a disaster. I was arrested for DUI. I had only been a mile from home—just off Highway 99 —but instead of heading there, I was on my way to jail. Washington State had a mandatory three-day sentence for DUI, so my car was towed, and my so-called freedom vanished. This time, I hadn't found a loophole.

Rock Bottom in Repeat

After serving my three-day sentence, I was released. Surprisingly, I felt grateful—for the forced detox, for the chance to clear my head. The police even called me a cab, and I went home feeling... different. That feeling didn't last long.

Still lost in thought, I took a short drive in my $300 car. I entered a bar, where the doorman greeted me. Minutes later, the first celebratory beer was already sliding down my throat. My trio of self-pity, intellect, and alcohol was missing their fourth member—crack. So, I went looking for it. As I turned the key in the ignition, a figure stepped into my headlights. It was the doorman. "Turn it off," he said, then introduced himself—not just as security, but as an off-duty police officer. I was arrested again. Within three hours of my release, I was back in jail.

It was February 19, 1991. In Washington State, a second DUI meant thirty days in jail and a suspended license. But there was a loophole—the system hadn't yet processed my first DUI from three days prior. Technically, on record, this was still my first offense. The officer booking me looked at me, shaking his head. "Didn't I just let you go?" I served another three days.

By the time I got out, I had lost my construction job. No-show, no-call for six days—there was nothing to explain. I needed to survive, so I started working day labor jobs. There were companies that hired workers—some legally, some off the books—and sent us to various job sites for a day's pay. The under-the-table jobs were the best. They paid cash, no taxes, and put more money in my hands. We called them "catch-outs." Everyone knew where to go to get hired—certain parking lots, like Lowe's, or specific street corners. The work was mostly construction: digging ditches, roofing, landscaping. Hard labor. But it didn't matter. I'd work, make my $20–$25, buy alcohol, smoke crack, and do it all over again whenever I needed cash.

One night, I was drinking at a bar with some guys from a job when a street couple joined us. We drank together, and soon, the topic of weed came up. "I know where to get some," I told them. They didn't know me from Adam, but I was their only connection to a dealer. To reassure them, I offered my driver's license as collateral, and they handed me $40. I went to my guy, gave him the money, and waited. He walked around the corner and never came back. I had just been beaten out of $40.

Returning to the bar, I told the couple what happened. They didn't believe me. The woman, furious, pressed me for answers. I wasn't about to start a fight over it. "Whatever," I muttered, ending my night right there. Then I went home.

From the High Seas to the Low Road

Working catch-outs wasn't a way forward for me. I knew there had to be a better way for an Ivy League-educated guy to make a decent wage. I figured if I just changed my geography once more, I could make things work. So, I went down to the docks and eventually landed a job on a fishing boat. The company flew me up to Dutch Harbor, Alaska, where I found myself processing black and pea cod. I don't like the smell or taste of fish, but there I was—low man on the totem pole, a true greenhorn—sorting and processing fish.

While retrieving a net, our boat hit a snag, and the steel cables snapped. We managed to pull the net back in, but it was missing the steel doors that keep the net open. The captain had no choice but to return to the harbor, where we were told it would be a week before the replacement parts arrived from Seattle. Worse yet, because we didn't have a full load, we didn't get paid. The money goes to the boat first. Frustrated, I went to the bar.

There, I met another Black man and explained my situation. He worked on a different boat and asked if I wanted a job with his crew. Excited by the opportunity, I grabbed my duffle bag and headed off with him. This time, we were after the coveted opilio—snow crabs. In Dutch Harbor, each captain sets the rules on whether his crew can drink during the season. Some boats are dry, but after our first haul, our captain handed each of us $100 and gave us one night to cut loose before we unloaded the boat.

At the bar, I was enjoying a cold beer when a prostitute approached, offering $100 blowjobs. While the idea sounded tempting, my beer was colder and better company. I didn't want to miss the boat, so after a few drinks, I returned and tried to find the most comfortable place to sleep—the captain's quarters. Hungover the next morning, I woke up wondering how many hundreds, or thousands, that prostitute had made that night.

As we offloaded the crab, a series of mistakes led the winch operator to drop a massive load—hundreds of pounds—into the sub-deck refrigerator where I was working. It barely missed one of the crew members. The cursing started as quickly as the blame, with "motherfuckers" and "fuck you" flying through the air like the chaotic gaggle of seagulls above us. Apparently, tempers run short on these stinky, cold, wet, hard-labor vessels.

Two guys were really going at it, and in my wisdom, I decided to step in and calm them down. What I didn't realize was that I had just broken an unwritten rule in Dutch Harbor: greenhorns don't exist. Their voices are nothing but farts in the wind. I should have kept my mouth shut and definitely shouldn't have gotten between two seasoned workers mid-fight.

My interjection infuriated one of them. He looked me dead in the eye—and spat in my face.

HE SPIT IN MY FACE.

For the second time in my life, my fist was against a man's face before I could think or blink. Unlike the time I snapped at Sam, I was now bigger, stronger, and knew how to throw a real punch. It landed clean, and I cold-cocked him. As he stumbled back, the crew jumped in, grabbing both of us. The captain stormed over, furious, siding with his trusted deckhand. Without hesitation, he kicked me off the boat.

With no job and nowhere to go, I called my mom. She told me I needed to come home anyway—a letter had arrived, and there was a warrant out for my arrest.

To my dismay, the couple from the bar—the ones I'd tried to buy weed for—had filed a police report, somehow concocting a story that made it look like I had stolen their $40. As proof, they had my driver's license, which I had stupidly forgotten to get back. That was enough for the police. Just like that, I picked up my first misdemeanor theft charge—for $40.

My mom helped me get back to Seattle, and I turned myself in at King County. I served a few days and was released at trial with time served. After that, I found myself drifting—jumping between missions, partying where I could, drinking, drugging, catching out, and living my insanity.

I'd moved and was sharing a place with these two white guys in the Green Lake district of Seattle. While walking around, I heard loud music and tracked it down to a house party. In true Ken fashion, I simply walked inside and began mingling. I had some weed on me, and this was a bunch of white kids. They offered to trade me acid for my weed, and I said okay. I had fun, got very drunk, and walked back home. The next morning, I wanted to smoke some weed and realized it was gone. I did, however, find a four-tab blotter of acid. I took a tab, and after a minute didn't feel anything, so I took another. I'd heard so much about the acid trip and felt I'd been stiffed with these bum drugs, so I took the other two tabs just a minute later. Try, try again. Before I could make it out of the bathroom, it hit me. It kicked me like a mule and left me curled up on the bathroom floor for the next six hours, begging God to allow me to come down from the high. My perception of reality had become so twisted and misshapen that I was terrified, pleading with God to allow me to have my reality back. It was a horrible experience, and I never touched acid again.

I arrived at a transfer station and waited for the next bus. There were only two other people, one of them a very cute white girl. When the bus arrived, only her and I got on the bus. When she got on the bus, I glanced in the young woman's purse and saw the only thing she had inside was a tampon. At that moment, she possessed a lot more than I did.

We sat adjacent each other and just struck up a conversation. She was also heading towards Seattle and asked me if I partied? Those were my magic words plus it was July 4th weekend. "Hell yeah. Where are you headed now?", I asked. We talked some more, and she said she'd get us a room. I was absolutely down for that. She was beautiful. Curious, I asked, "how old are you?" She then said she was 18 yet so I needed to help her with the room. It was a long bus ride and she started sharing with me her life's story. She'd come from a small, white town in rural Washington, called Gold Bar.

We got off the bus near the Black Angus Inn and she handed me a $20 bill. She told me to go inside so I went and sat at the bar. I was happy as a clam because I now had something to drink. A few minutes later I heard a high pitched voice saying "Kenny, Kenny." As I turned around, she was standing at the door, too young to enter the bar at 18 and motioned for me to come to her. She discreetly handed me $100. It was 2pm and I knew there were very few things she could be doing to get that kind of money that quickly and I now understood why she didn't need to carry money on her; she was her own ATM. She turned around and disappeared again as I went back to the bar. The bartender remained ambivalent, monkey see/monkey blind, as she returned 15 or 20 minutes later. "Kenny, Kenny. Here!" Reaching out, she smiled and handed me another $100. I went and got us a room then left to find some crack.

She didn't smoke crack but was ok being around me while I did. She drank a little but not heavily. She told me her name was Siri but her street name was Sunshine and I accepted the job as her pimp. Our conversation continued as did the one in my head. There weren't many people there in Gold Bar and families kept things close. She explained from early on, she explained she'd been a tool in her family and had been repeatedly sexually abused until she left after feeling unwanted or loved. She'd learned to take care of herself in many ways and, she said, had been on the streets prostituting since she was 12. It was easy for her since she was fully developed, pretty, unwittingly experienced, white, and young. Gold Bar had already taught her she was an object of sexual desire and release, so she just went with it.

I knew I was wrong but between her and the crack, my logic and reasoning had already been disarmed. I was in my "fuck its" and she was an opportunity. Drunk and high, we had sex.

The Business of Control

It was 1991, and my life with Sunshine began. When I got back to Seattle, she already knew the ho strolls—the well-established circuits where prostitutes and pimps operated. At the time, Seattle had four main strolls: South Tacoma, Downtown Seattle, Highway 99 North between 45th and 110th, and the SeaTac area. We'd work one area for a while, sleeping in nearby motels until the police started cracking down. When the heat became too much, we'd move. Over time, we learned their patterns, just as they adapted to ours. The working girls shared information just like the cops did, and this constant back-and-forth became a choreographed dance between the streets and law enforcement.

I had never been a pimp before, but Sunshine didn't mind —she knew I'd learn quickly. On the streets, there were two types of pimps, categorized by how they controlled their girls. The first was the gorilla pimp—the heavy-handed, violent enforcers often depicted in movies. When their girls stepped out of line, they'd use physical force to bring them back. These men (and sometimes women) were part of what we called the Slap-A-Ho clique. Then, there were men like me. I wasn't violent. My demeanor was disarming and welcoming —strong and protective, yet forceful and kind. In all my years, I recall striking a woman only once, and even then, it was a single swat on the butt when she had completely stepped out of line. My approach was different. I controlled women emotionally and psychologically. I was a manipulator, not a brute. I belonged to the Save-A-Ho clique.

The women who worked the streets also fell into two main categories. Some operated under the supervision and protection of a pimp—though many would call them their "boyfriend," avoiding the reality of their situation. Others were independent, known as "free agents." Within the game, there were also three distinct modes of prostitution. The most common, yet least desirable, was incidental prostitution—random, one-off transactions, much like a restaurant owner constantly trying to put new customers in seats every day. The second mode involved building a roster of regulars—men the girls could call when they needed quick cash. These regulars provided a degree of stability, knowing they had options available. The third and most lucrative mode was securing a sugar daddy—a man who provided full financial support in exchange for a long-term arrangement. In another time or place, these women might have been called mistresses, but in this world, they were simply owned.

Controlling the women was easy. In all my years, I never met a working girl who hadn't started as a victim of sexual abuse. The abuser was often a family member, a boyfriend of the mother, or someone trusted within their household. The trauma always started young. How they responded to it—and how the people around them reacted—determined whether they fell into the life. Their mental vulnerability led to their physical vulnerability. Many had detached from their bodies long before they ever worked the streets.

By the time they became prostitutes, they no longer saw sex as something intimate or meaningful. Their bodies were simply tools. They performed whatever act a john paid for, while their minds disconnected from the experience. Their ability to dissociate was stunning—almost mechanical—but it was the only way they could reconcile their past trauma with their present reality. This emotional detachment also dictated how they chose to operate. A girl's perception of herself and her past abuse determined whether she needed a gorilla, a "boyfriend," or had the confidence to work alone.

The streets were ruthless, but they had a system. And I was learning exactly how to play the game.

Siri loved me. I knew and felt it. She'd do anything for her "Kenny," and I could see she loved me 100 percent. Besides Jacob and my mom, I still wasn't sure if I knew how to give love back or even how to receive love. If protecting her, sleeping with her, laughing with her, and grabbing her favorite McDonald's Quarter Pounders were the transactions she identified as love, then sure, I loved her. I definitely knew I cared for her.

My greatest love, though—the one I'd do anything for, my ultimate—was crack cocaine. Nothing and no one stood between me and my love for long. Our consensually non-monogamous relationship was unbreakable.

Siri and I were on the second floor of a motel near the Space Needle in the summer of '91 when I wanted some crack. Three gangbangers from the Rolling 60's Crip gang, operating nearby, came up to our room to sell me the drugs and saw Siri lying on the bed. One said, "Hey, check this out, bro. We'll give you three if we can kick it with baby doll for a bit." There were many gangbangers moving through the area from Los Angeles to deal drugs in a growing Seattle market.

Siri was a moneymaker. She produced results and was thus a coveted commodity. Every good pimp desires a moneymaker, especially one who requires minimal care or instruction. I turned from the thugs, looked at Siri, and asked, "Hey, will you take care of this for me?" She said okay, and I left them to it.

I came back an hour and a half later and opened the door, only to be immediately kicked out. One of the thugs said, "We not done yet," and closed the door in my face. I went out to smoke and returned about an hour later. When I opened the door again, the look on her face became forever emblazoned in my mind. She loved me and accepted me as her protector, yet I'd left her with those wolves. I'd abandoned her, allowing her to become a mere sexual tool—a release for strangers—when she had trusted me to keep her safe. As our eyes met, the emotion conveyed in her expression struck my soul. I had failed her and was deeply disappointed in myself.

Things between us were never the same after that. Sure, I was her pimp—her "Kenny"—but she knew she also had to fend for herself. I'd allowed her to be violated, and at some deep level, I wasn't sure if she could forgive that betrayal of trust. She continued working and even secured some other girls for me.

There are worlds that exist outside of what normal eyes can see. People always talk about alternate dimensions but seem oblivious to the ones that exist here on earth. On their way home from work, they're thinking about the traffic they're in, picking up the kids, getting dinner ready, dealing with their spouse, the annoying in-law, or the hot shower and bed they can't wait to get into. They are blind to the street life that surrounds them.

It's an entire ecosystem. They don't see the drug game being played. They can't see the world where parents allow their young sons and daughters to be sexually abused and tell them to keep quiet—or worse, when little kids are passed around as payment for an outstanding debt. Many people are ignorant and reckless when they kick their "fast" girls out of the house, never bothering to ask what caused that behavior in the first place. Perhaps, if people cared enough to see or learn, they would discover their little girl was being abused by her older brother and his friends, sending her into a spiraling identity crisis. Perhaps they'd care more if they knew putting her on the streets for being a chronic runaway or "fast" would result in her turning tricks while her peers were studying eighth-grade science. Maybe, or maybe not.

Siri saw different dimensions. She knew different worlds. All the working girls did, and I learned to open my eyes and mind as well. One day she was approached by the owner of a very popular restaurant in the area. He wanted to party with her by having a foursome with her and two other young girls aged 12 and 14. She agreed and the price was $1,000 for the three girls for three days. They met up and headed out on a Saturday. By Tuesday, I really needed some money. Siri had not returned yet so I called the client at his house which surprised him. "Who is this?" he asked. "Don't worry about it. Is Siri there? Put Siri on the phone", I demanded. She answered and I told her I needed some money. She met me at McDonalds and broke me off $100 before quickly returning to her date. As the third day passed, she did not shown up. I called the client again looking for Siri. He told me she and the other girls had gone off with Chocolate, an 18-year-old prostitute well-known on the streets. I'd just lost my moneymaker.

A Dangerous Spiral

Siri and I would get back together, then off again, several times. She'd come back to find her "Kenny," and I'd be grateful to have her. One day, while at a motel, she went out to work. I fell asleep but was awakened by loud banging on the door. Opening it, I found police officers standing there, asking if I knew a girl named Siri. They indicated that they wanted to talk to me about "promotion of solicitation of prostitution." I didn't even know that was the legal term. They explained she'd been arrested for prostitution, was underage, and had identified me as her pimp. I knew it wasn't a good situation, but I did as I'd learned to do when faced with overwhelming authority and consequences—I lied. Internally, I couldn't believe she'd given them my name and location. I was seething, but that had to wait. The immediate danger was standing in front of me, threatening my freedom. Seeing that I was unwilling to incriminate myself, the officers eventually left. I closed the door, said a few choice words, and went back to sleep. I figured I might as well get whatever rest I could, because the motel manager, upon seeing the police presence, had already informed me that I could only stay through the rest of the night. Bringing police attention was always a black flag at motels.

A few hours later, there came another knock at the door. Shit! My mind began racing but, with nowhere to go, I answered. "Kenny!" Siri exclaimed, standing there, seemingly genuinely happy to see me. Excitedly, she asked, "Would you like to meet my mom?"

Incredulous, I responded, "Fuck no, I don't want to meet your mom!"

She turned around, waved, and called out, "Bye, Mom!" I stood confused as a woman waved back, then drove away. Apparently, when the police realized Siri was underage, they'd called her mom, who immediately drove the hour to pick her up. Beyond belief, Siri's mom had dropped her back off to her pimp. Siri had been busted by an undercover John. Now she, her mom, and I stood for judgment as Jesus's eight words commanded: "Let he who is without sin cast the first stone." We were living in a different world—a fifth, sixth, or tenth alternate reality. Who'd cast the first stone? Siri and I returned to our on-again, off-again routine, mostly off, because she soon disappeared again.

Having lost Siri as a dependable source of income, I returned to day labor in Seattle's University District to support my habit. I went on a catch-out construction job with a guy and a small crew of eses. We were remodeling a house in a nice middle-class neighborhood, which required some travel. The boss liked our crew's work ethic and wanted to make sure we were all there the next day, so he allowed us to stay on the vacant job site overnight. A few crew members and I went out and bought alcohol, getting drunk together. We soon ran out of alcohol and money, but I had an idea. Grabbing a long steel pry bar—a monkey bar—I went to a nearby house that was clearly unoccupied. Yes, I could tell someone lived there, but they hadn't been home in a while, likely using it as a vacation home. My Mexican crew counterparts thought I was crazy but sat chatting among themselves while I completely removed a framed window from the side of that house, out of public view, and set it aside. I climbed my drunken self into the house and immediately began searching for valuables. All told, I found a gun, some jewelry, and a couple of nearly empty prescription pill bottles in the medicine cabinet. I knew I'd messed up by breaking in, but the damage was already done. I left, went and got some dope, then returned.

The other crew members were still there, so I found another nearby house whose garage door was left slightly open. Drunk and high, I pried it open the rest of the way, slid under, and promptly fell asleep in the garage.

Someone from the crew snitched on me. The boss was livid and called the police. Knowing this, I decided to commit my first violation of the cardinal rule of the streets: never tell on yourself. I went to the Seattle jail and turned myself in. Though still high, I had the sense to dump the gun before entering the police station. I confessed I'd committed a burglary, handed over the jewelry, and was arrested. Back in jail, I went to the bathroom, still hungover, and started vomiting. To my amazement, I looked down and found two balloons of heroin on the ground. Apparently, someone else had brought these in—two balloon shots of heroin about a quarter the size of a dime—but had left them there for whatever reason. Perhaps a guard or someone else had walked in, causing them to ditch them quickly; maybe they intended to return later and retrieve the drugs.

Reaching back, I pulled out the little bag of pills I'd hastily wrapped up and shoved inside my backside. Removing everything from its respective bag, I started swallowing. I took the pills, having no earthly idea what they were, along with both bags of black tar heroin. Good God—I was as high as I'd ever been, and I'd managed it from inside the jail.

CHAPTER 7: MY REFLECTIONS

Rock bottom has layers. Every time I thought I had hit my lowest point, I discovered a new depth. Sleeping in missions, selling my body, losing jobs, watching my mother almost die —I kept thinking, *This has to be it.* But addiction doesn't let you just wake up one day and decide you're done. It drags you deeper, makes you justify more, until the things you swore you'd never do become just another Tuesday. The real bottom isn't a place; it's the moment you stop digging.

1. **The Cycle Doesn't Break Itself** - Homelessness isn't just about lacking a roof over your head—it's a mindset, a rhythm, a survival pattern that traps you in its grip. The missions, the motels, the street hustle—it all becomes routine. Once something feels routine, it stops feeling temporary, and that's the real danger. It's easy to convince yourself that the next shelter bed, the next handout, the next drink is just a stepping-stone instead of another loop in the cycle.
2. **Shelter Isn't Stability** - Missions offer food, a mat, maybe even structure—but they don't offer transformation. You can move through the ranks,

follow the rules, even find a sense of order, but unless something inside shifts, you're just existing in another kind of holding pattern. The reality is, no system, no program, no shelter can force you to change. They can only give you space to realize you need to.

3. **Numbness is Its Own Kind of Prison** - When I saw my mother in that hospital bed after her suicide attempt, the only thing I felt was...nothing. That's the most dangerous place to be—not rage, not sorrow, but absolute indifference. Because once you stop feeling, you stop caring. Once you stop caring, you stop trying. The streets, the shelters, the cycle—it all becomes a slow-motion free fall. And the worst part is, you don't even brace for impact.
4. **Prostitution is More Than a Transaction** - Selling yourself isn't just about money. It's about what you're willing to trade for comfort, safety, or the illusion of control. Whether it's a sugar daddy offering a bed, a quick fix to quiet the pain, or a relationship built on manipulation, the currency isn't just cash—it's your sense of self. The moment you justify the exchange, you start losing track of who you were before you started making deals.
5. **You Can't Outrun Yourself** - Seattle, Port Townsend, Alaska—it didn't matter where I went; I always took myself with me. A new city, a new job,

a new opportunity—none of it meant anything if I wasn't willing to face the person looking back at me in the mirror. Change isn't about a different location; it's about a different mindset. No matter how many fresh starts you get, the past has a way of catching up when you refuse to do the work.

CHAPTER 8
DESTRUCTIVE PATTERNS & HARDENING CONSEQUESES

I was arraigned the next day, informed of my rights and what to expect. A few days later, I appeared before the judge and pleaded guilty to felony burglary. I didn't realize just how foolish I'd been until the sober tone of the judge filled me with dread. He explained that the burglary I'd committed could have resulted in harm to human life, chastising me by saying I needed to be thankful to God that no one was home. I mused silently about whether judges grow tired of seeing low-level criminals and become indifferent themselves, catching their own case of "fuck it." The judge's voice interrupted my thoughts as he asked if I understood I'd committed a Class A felony, which carried a mandatory minimum sentence of five years in prison. In Washington State, it didn't matter that no one was home. What mattered was that someone could have been home, potentially forcing me to harm them, thus categorizing my crime as violent. Whatever alternate reality I was living in or silent musings I was having suddenly vanished.

For me, one aspect of granting grace is forgiveness. It's the allowance and space for the human condition; a measured response to transgressions rather than complete retribution or annihilation. We are imperfect by nature, and without grace, the entire world would cycle repeatedly through mass extinctions, failed experiments needing to restart from scratch. There are entities capable of affecting you in time or space—one of them being a judge. They can dictate how long you exist and under what conditions. The reality was that I stood in front of another human—a judge—with the authority to impose a $50,000 fine and imprison me for at least five years.

Because it was my first offense, the judge considered my Dartmouth background, work history, my lack of criminal record, and my accountable nature. I didn't even have tattoos. Everyone knows real criminals must have tattoos. With grace, he looked at me and said I wasn't a criminal but I did need help. He convicted me of the felony but sentenced me to 30 days in jail to clean up, followed by inpatient drug addiction treatment. In addition, I had to complete two years of intensive probation. He had taken it easy on me. After serving my month, I was released on probation.

Probation and Parole

Probation and parole are both forms of supervised release from incarceration, but they have distinct differences. Probation is a court-ordered alternative to imprisonment, typically granted as part of a sentence. It allows individuals to remain in the community under supervision, subject to conditions such as regular check-ins, drug testing, and compliance with court orders. Parole, however, is the early release from felony incarceration, granted by a parole board after the individual has served part of their sentence in prison. Parole allows individuals to serve the remainder of their sentence in the community under similar supervision. However, unlike probation, parole typically applies to individuals who have already served prison time and are eligible for early release due to good behavior or rehabilitation. I had served time in jail but not prison. I had been clean—or at least in between using—since those keistered drugs, and now I walked freely amongst the community as long as I stayed in compliance.

I called Sam. I reached out to my father and said, “Hey, Dad. I’m like you now—I’m a convicted felon.” I thought perhaps at this moment he’d finally see some value in me or recognize something that bonded us together. I’d spent 11 of my first 17 years with him and was still searching for his acceptance as his son. He broke the silence by replying, “You’re a fucking idiot. What a waste,” and hung up the phone.

Knowing I was about to start my treatment, I went searching for Siri. I found her at the Geisha Inn off Aurora Avenue, in a motel room with three other young working girls. She was happy to see me and greeted me with her signature “Kenny!” She wanted things to return to how they were, but I told her I couldn’t be her pimp anymore. In jail, I’d had time to reconsider my decisions. Remaining the Black pimp of a young white girl and her friends was not a smart move. If the judge wanted to scare me straight, it had worked. Plus, she'd inadvertently given me up once already; promotion of solicitation would violate my probation and could send me away for a very long time. I'd done dumb things, but I wasn't stupid.

However, despite acknowledging the risk, I still needed money and justified that while Siri was now a free agent, she should still break me off some cash. I told her as much, and she agreed. I left, but when I returned the next morning to collect, the other girls said she'd left with a message that she wasn't coming back. It was the first time she directly disobeyed me, triggering an angry emotional spiral. I began tweaking badly. I had $20 to my name, so I sought some crack. I gave my $20 to a friend and asked him to get crack for me. He didn't come back. He'd beat me for the $20. I didn't want to get caught buying drugs on the street, so I said, "Forget it, I'll smoke tomorrow." I fell asleep, and when I woke up the next day, the tweaking feeling was gone. For the first time since my initial high, I had managed to stave off the overwhelming compulsion for crack cocaine. This motivated me and instilled hope. I'd hit a milestone and deeply craved sobriety, developing a healthy fear of the pain on the other side of relapse.

I was obligated to a treatment center called Cedar Hills in Seattle—a 90-day inpatient facility run by King County. It held prostitutes, hustlers, drug addicts, and many low-level criminals from varied backgrounds. It was a serene place, complete with beautiful landscaping and ducks swimming nearby on calm waters. Occasionally, the smell from the nearby King County landfill would waft on the breeze, but that could be ignored as we played basketball or conversed amongst ourselves. It was a co-ed facility, though men and women had separate dormitories, divided by trees. It provided a welcome respite from street life turmoil, and we jokingly called our therapeutic interactions "jungle therapy." Those woods were filled with whispers of sexual exploits.

I met Stephanie there, my first "treatment romance." Temporary hookups in treatment were common—almost something to look forward to, connecting with relatable people equally needy for companionship who shared struggles as harrowing as my own. Stephanie was a beautifully-hearted lesbian who fell in love with me. She and I loved laughing together. Though our romance began within treatment center walls, it continued outside them. Our relationship explored honesty; I became comfortable pointing out women I found attractive as we walked down the street, and she'd discuss what she also found appealing in those same women. Amazingly, she had no interest in men beyond me.

A New Path: Modeling & Mistakes

I started lifting weights and getting in shape after deciding to see if I could get back into modeling. While at the gym, I met a white guy named Matthew, who also wanted to get into modeling, so we became workout partners. At that time, there were three main agencies in Seattle: Seattle Models Guild (SMG), Book Agency, and a smaller one. SMG was the biggest agency in town, having been around the longest—they were considered the Cadillac of the industry.

At SMG, I met a woman who thought I had great potential. I introduced her to my friend Matthew, and she became very interested in him as well. Having attended modeling school, I understood there were different looks for male models. There were looks I couldn't pull off, like the California beach/surfer look. Another was the After Hours look—similar to George Clooney in a tuxedo or the Dos Equis actor. Then there was the Continental look, typically featuring white men, though occasionally Black or African models with European features. At modeling school, the owner had told me I had great potential for the "Sears Catalog" look—an All-American, square style. I looked very innocent, had no tattoos, was handsome, had dimples, stood 6'1.5", weighed 190 lbs, and was perfectly shaped for a 44 regular suit size.

The agencies had books filled with photos of their models—headshot-style—much like adoption agencies in the 1960s, when Mom picked me out of the lineup. These books were for buyers seeking models, featuring only black-and-white headshots since buyers already knew the features and looks they desired. They didn't need to see your body because the agency screened for size and shape. The woman at SMG invited us and scheduled a book photoshoot. Matthew and I began working out even harder to prepare for our headshots. I was in the best shape of my life and thought everything looked great—I just needed to get my hair relaxed a little bit.

There were many gay men at Cedar Hills, many of whom did makeup and hair. The top stylist there was a good friend of mine, so I asked if he could do my hair. He told me to stop by his apartment, and he'd take care of me. I visited him on a Sunday, explaining I just needed my hair relaxed slightly. About five other effeminate gay men—Black and Puerto Rican—were there, having a good time. My friend had a client at that moment and couldn't do my hair, but he suggested I ask one of the others. Turning to the group, who had clearly heard our conversation, I asked, "Okay, who wants to do me?" In near-perfect harmony, they shouted, "Oh, I'll do you!" The room erupted in laughter. I quickly clarified, "Do my hair."

The laughter and banter continued, but one guy agreed to help me. He escorted me to the kitchen to apply the relaxer. He put the product in and instructed me to let him know when it started to burn. I have a high pain tolerance and wasn't concerned about the burn—I just needed a slight relaxing before the photoshoot. The chemicals break down hair bonds and can burn the scalp. When he came to check on me, I assured him I was fine. About twenty minutes later, my scalp started tingling, and I told him. He came back, removed the plastic cap, and exclaimed, "Oooooh, shit!" My hair was slicked straight back—I looked like a young Black version of Miami Heat owner Pat Riley. I was immediately depressed. This guy had completely ruined my hair, and I knew it would take a while to grow back curly. It sucked, but there was nothing I could do except continue working out and wait.

I cut my hair off and graduated from Cedar Hills after 90 days. It was a great day. They had a little ceremony, and I was appreciative to earn my certificate. I felt a sense of accomplishment and finally believed I had a stable enough platform to stand on. A few days later, I met Matthew to work out, and he excitedly told me he'd been booked for a modeling gig in Italy. I was ecstatic for him because he'd worked hard, and Europe was a huge opportunity. Although I wouldn't have been able to travel to Europe anyway because I was on probation, I still recognized I'd had a setback. It would take a few months for my hair to grow back, and I knew I'd missed an opportunity. I had messed up again! It was emotionally triggering, but my compulsion to use was tamped down. I'd survived another one. Good job, Ken—you can do this.

One day, Matthew, another friend named Mark, and I all went to get tested for HIV together. Aside from one wart once in my life, I'd never had any indication of a sexually transmitted disease, but HIV and AIDS were rampant at the time, with marketing campaigns heavily targeting gay men. The waiting period for results was terrifying—I don't know if I'd ever been so nervous in my life. Back then, results took weeks, and that fear motivated me to try treatment again. I went to a halfway house—what today would be called transitional housing—and joined another outpatient program.

Mark got his results first: he had full-blown AIDS. Then Matthew's results came back negative, and mine also came back negative. I felt sad for Mark, yet relieved for myself. With the help of Reverend Steve Johnson at Therapeutic Services, I stayed sober for the next two years. I made amends with the church for what I'd done, and they extended grace to me, helping me stay clean. It was the spring of 1992, and as EMF sang, my life was unbelievable.

Enjoying Sobriety

I began enjoying sobriety, and I was also enjoying my time with Stephanie—until my eyes and thoughts began wandering again. Our relationship lasted a few months, but like everyone else in my life, she soon fell victim to my near-serial non-monogamy. I've always held that speaking in clichés is one of the laziest forms of communication. Sometimes, though, a cliché captures a moment so accurately and succinctly that it's the most appropriate response. In my case, "hurt people hurt people." I ended our journey together on Valentine's Day—another unkind act committed by a lost man.

Soon after, Stephanie tried to commit suicide. She was an emotionally triggered slasher, and after I broke up with her, she attempted to end her life by overdosing on prescription meds and cutting herself. I was troubled by what she'd done but maintained my sobriety, as I'd largely lost the compulsion to use. I stayed in the gym, avoided shady environments, and kept out of trouble. I was back on track for the first time in years.

One night, I went to a club with a friend, and we began playing pool. This place had a nice ambiance, large TVs with sports playing, and some good options for us to look at. We noticed a few attractive girls there and were approached by two cute ones. The usual obligatory small talk ensued for a while. We played pool, and all was well.

The music ended, and the girl who had been talking to me, Lora, asked if I wanted to go home with her. It didn't take long before I was in her apartment, and we were having sex. To my absolute astonishment, she explained that she was leaving for Egypt the next day with her sister and handed me the keys to her apartment and her car. I thought I'd died and gone to heaven. There was no trick—she was just genuinely kind-hearted and trusted me immediately. She returned from Egypt, and our romance continued. She worked at Fred Hutchinson Cancer Research Center, and I excelled at my new job with a company called Pro Displays. Together, we started doing Amway, engaging in multi-level marketing with a group called World Wide Dream Builders. This was 1992, and to me, it was a continuation of my training and expansion of knowledge in sales and marketing.

I met a woman named Kathy in the fragrance department of Nordstrom. After meeting her, an inconvenient truth surfaced in my consciousness: I didn't love Lora. With that knowledge, I began augmenting our relationship with little forays with other women. I'd also begun talking to my high school sweetheart again, whispering about a potential union, perhaps even returning to Anchorage and getting married.

At the same time, while working out at the gym, I saw a woman named Chrissy doing deadlifts. I was impressed. Deadlifts had always been one of my favorite exercises, and seeing her potential—but also some flaws in her technique —I approached and offered some input. Before the day was over, I was at her house making out. I was honest and explained that I had a girlfriend. She respected that and never let our sessions move to intercourse. At one point, I had four different women I was involved with while living with Lora, and the deceit was eroding my soul daily. I questioned my morality and ethics, as I was clearly using Lora's love to provide myself stability and support in sobriety. Additionally, I hid elements of my past and present from Lora, feeling unable to be completely transparent. I couldn't bring myself to tell her I'd exchanged sexual favors with men for shelter and money. She held me in such high esteem, and I was borrowing her view of me since I largely lacked esteem of my own. That was true with all of them—each filled some void within me and allowed me to feel more complete. However, I could never entirely fill the void, and eventually, I became emotionally overwhelmed with guilt.

Chrissy and I continued talking as good friends, often meeting for lunch and conversation, while Kathy and I visited occasionally, and Lora provided my stability. Chrissy approached me one day to let me know she was pregnant. I knew the baby's father because we worked out together at the gym. He was already married with kids and wanted nothing to do with Chrissy—she had just been a hookup for him. It was all a bit much, and I was emotionally torn, but looking at Chrissy, I offered to help and support her through the birth. It was an unconventional offer and caught Chrissy by surprise, but she still declined. It was her responsibility, and she stood up to the challenge, unwilling to burden someone else.

Stretched On All Sides

Lora and her sister went on another trip out of Seattle. Stressed from the various strings pulling me in different directions, I relapsed. My almost three-year walk with sobriety ended, and I was back into alcohol-fueled crack addiction. I had the keys to Lora and her sister's places and began using both as party houses while they were gone. By the time Lora returned, I was in full-blown addiction again, though I hid it from Chrissy. Upon her return, Lora was beside herself at what I'd done and who I'd become. She didn't recognize me anymore, and we parted ways. She kicked me out, and I moved in with Mark, the friend who had AIDS. Mark's brain and body were deteriorating rapidly, and this beautiful Victorian home in the U District was being used as a hospice, primarily for gay men dying of AIDS. His group was gracious enough to offer me a temporary room.

While there, in transition, I reached out to Chrissy again and offered to marry her. It seemed like a rational decision: she needed a father for her child, and I needed stability. We liked each other, and logically, it made sense to me. Out of respect to the AIDS group and a desire to recapture my sobriety, I quit cold turkey and got clean again while convincing Chrissy that our union made perfect sense. I didn't want her to work anymore, as a sober Ken was a good provider. She'd had the baby, Joey, and I enjoyed being around him very much. I felt I would be the father I'd always desired and never had. I would take care of both of them, provided she agreed to three things: I wanted her not to work, to provide a home-cooked meal, and to provide sex. She agreed, and in December 1994, I flew out to Sacramento, then drove north to Marysville, California, just outside Yuba City.

There wasn't a strong romance between Chrissy and me, at least not in the way I imagined a relationship should be. Though we'd fooled around a few times, we'd never had sex, as she didn't want to while I was with another woman or before marriage. Still, I enjoyed Joey and her attention. I went to meet her family, pulling up to a large, 1,000-plus-acre estate with its own private airstrip. Through her mother's marriage, her family owned a Busch distributorship and were very well-off. Her stepfather greeted me before the ladies walked away chatting among themselves. He said, "Let's go for a talk." We walked over to an airplane hangar where he had two aircraft parked. We got in one, he fired it up, and we took off. The trees whizzed by beneath us, and I appreciated the sun—but there was a problem. I was sure her dad was going to push me out of the plane over some remote ravine or something. I couldn't enjoy the flight. We returned home safely, and conversations continued. Chrissy and her mother argued often, but I was very cool with her. My future mother-in-law's energy and mine seemed to align. Indeed, things were looking great. From the outside, no one would know Joey wasn't mine, and I was okay with that. My mom pointed out the convenient resemblance between Joey and me, similar to how people always said I looked like my mom. Though technically loveless, I believe our relationship was in good faith, and we both wanted it to work.

We got married that February in a small ceremony at the

estate. A few of her family and friends came, as well as my mom and my good friend Roy. My mother was there to support me. We were newlyweds, and I was embracing my newly acquired role as a dad. As a wedding gift, her parents gave us a condo—yes, gave us, no rent!—where we both began to acclimate to our new arrangement. I enjoyed my time with her, and she seemingly enjoyed mine as well, albeit awkwardly at times as we searched for how the puzzle pieces fit together. One night she denied me sex, and before I knew it, the self-talk began: "She doesn't love you. She doesn't desire you. You're just here as a placeholder for her baby's father. If she loved you, she'd take care of your needs. Your mom was right; she just wants to be with you because, to the outside world, you look like you could be the father." I didn't know what to say to her after that point, and I definitely didn't know what to do, so we went to sleep.

Down The Rabbit Hole

Early that Saturday morning, I needed space to think. I needed to change my environment. I searched my mind feverishly but couldn't recall a single instance—not one—of her saying she loved me. What was this that I felt for her and Joey? Was it love? A familiar feeling crept in. I hadn't stayed in a program because I felt secure, having survived staying clean for so long while with Lora and having quit again cold turkey to make this work with Chrissy. I figured this new role as husband and father would be enough reason to keep me clean, but now I was struggling. I called my best friend

Matthew to explain how rejected I felt that my wife didn't want to have sex with me. I felt unwanted. I'll never forget his prophetic words: "Ken, you're going to relapse if you don't deal with this anguish and pain." I was having one hell of an emotionally triggering event.

I told Chrissy I was going to the store. I walked out of the condo and never went back. I went to Sacramento, where I relapsed on crack. Then I moved in with my mom, who lived in Reno, Nevada, filed for divorce, and went into a major depression. I was prescribed Paxil and began taking it.

My mom had already picked up a new job as a professor at the University of Nevada, Reno School of Nursing, and I was happy to be near her again. It wasn't all rosy for her, though. Shortly after arriving, she and other nurses began experiencing discrimination. My mom had even been called a racial slur while talking with someone at the university. Having had enough, she helped organize a group that became known as The White Orchids. They sued the university, eventually winning their case.

Me? I hopscotched between addiction and recovery, jumping from outpatient treatment centers, missions, and street life in Reno. I dabbled in pimping, prostitution, and smoking crack. Little did I know, I'd been playing in the minor leagues. I discovered a new dimension—a seeming leveling-up of street knowledge and experience—while falling further down the addiction hole.

Reno was a different scene, with a lot of gang activity surrounding the drug trade. Like in Seattle, most of the major players in Reno were visitors from California. I quickly learned that the street game here revolved mainly around motels, where the majority of drug transactions, prostitution, and general criminal activities took place.

By 1997, I found myself living in an apartment building with about 20 rooms, at least 18 of which were occupied by crack smokers and alcoholics. One day, I walked down the hall, turned the corner, and saw two guys jaw-jacking, arguing intensely. One of the men was a familiar young D-boy from Oakland—an area we referred to as "Town Business." In certain circles, people asked if you were from "town business," indicating an Oakland affiliation. Everyone knew to leave those guys alone. They weren't typical gangsters like the Seattle or Reno crews—Oakland guys were hardened killers.

The other man in the argument was a young, bullheaded addict who was a local. As other residents began coming out due to the commotion, the D-boy grew increasingly upset at the blatant disrespect coming from this obvious crackhead. As their voices rose, the D-boy's shirt lifted slightly, and I spotted a pistol tucked into the small of his back. I interjected, telling the local guy to back off and "chill the fuck out," but he kept going. Though I knew both of them, I tried my best not to get too involved—bullets don't have names. Fearing for my safety and not wanting to witness a shooting, I left the area and found somewhere calmer to smoke. To this day, I have no idea what happened afterward beyond my getting high.

I was fully engrossed in my addiction at that point and supporting myself entirely. I had no girls working for me, couldn't obtain or keep a job, and had repeatedly burned bridges that could have led me back into recovery. I was alone on the streets, lacking any support system except for my friend Matthew, who had moved back to Gardena near Century Avenue in LA.

Eventually, my situation in Reno deteriorated severely. I was so sick and intoxicated that I feared dying. Desperate, I checked myself into a detox center for those suffering from acute alcohol or drug intoxication. The facility, run by Washoe County, was familiar—I'd been there two or three times before. Their role was essentially medical monitoring, preventing me from dying on the streets. The stay involved 72 hours in a hospital bed with food and amenities while my body recovered. If I had chosen, I could have transferred from detox to a treatment center. At the time, I was malnourished and dehydrated—common symptoms of acute alcoholism and crack addiction.

While detoxing, I received a $500 check as back pay from a previous job. With some money in hand, I decided to fly to LA to meet up with Matthew and relax. Within hours of leaving detox, I began drinking again on the plane. Arriving in LA, I approached a couple of brothers, offering them $50 to drive me to Matthew's place. They dropped me off at his home in Gardena. I bought a few 40oz beers and sat on Matthew's front porch, waiting for him to come home from work. The urge for crack returned, and with about $300 remaining, I figured I'd buy some. Since this was my first visit to LA and the neighborhood, I naively asked one of Matthew's neighbors to buy the crack for me. I gave him $100, and he walked off. By the time Matthew arrived, the guy hadn't returned. Matthew shook his head, essentially calling me an idiot for being so trusting and allowing the neighbor to beat me out of $100.

LA was the epicenter of crack cocaine at the time, known for offering the greatest quantity and quality for your dollar. Matthew had an excellent connection, so I gave him the remaining $200 to buy more. He soon returned with a solid chunk of crack nearly half the size of my fist. We stared at it excitedly, like kids on Christmas, eager to dive in.

We started smoking around 5 p.m. that Friday evening, taking hit after hit of crack nonstop every 15–20 minutes. Without needing food or drink, Matthew and I smoked continuously until the next evening. Finally, Matthew tapped out. He needed to come down and rest, and he wanted to sleep. Still floating in the clouds, I watched as he disappeared into his room, taking and hiding the remaining crack with him.

Coming Down Hard

It was 3 p.m. on a Saturday afternoon in Matthew's hood. He'd fallen asleep in his apartment, which was essentially unfurnished, leaving me alone with just beer and the high I was enjoying. I started searching for where he'd hidden the crack, all while pushing the pipe, which still had a ton of purified dope in it. I went into his closet and began checking his coat pockets, where I found roughly a one-inch-square piece of solid crack.

I took the crack into the bathroom and made the second biggest mistake of my life—second only to having smoked crack in the first place. I'd been pushing this pipe while searching for the crack but hadn't lit it. It had been about 45 minutes since my last hit, and I wanted a strong pick-me-up to get back on top. I broke off a substantial chunk and slid it onto the Brillo pad, which already had an insane amount of pure cocaine on it. I took a very deep hit. Within 10 seconds, I knew I had likely taken too much. Within 15–20 seconds, I knew beyond a shadow of a doubt that I was the highest I'd ever been in my life! I rocketed past my four-tab acid trip like a hypersonic missile on methamphetamine. Within 30 seconds, my first auditory hallucination began. It sounded like the introduction to Marvin Gaye's *What's Going On* looped in my head at maximum volume, accompanied by people talking all around me in every direction. There was a literal party of about 20 people in my head, but I was completely alone. Next, the walls started moving and melting, morphing and reshaping around me.

There is a brief moment when someone who has taken too much of a drug realizes they've messed up. I was well beyond that point, already freaking out when the tactile hallucinations began. Without warning, bugs started crawling all over me. I couldn't see them, but I felt them everywhere. Around that time, I became acutely aware that my heart was beating louder and faster than it ever had before. I had no frame of reference to compare it to; I just knew it wasn't good at all. Panicked, I turned the shower full blast on cold and—likely within one or two minutes of taking that single hit—I jumped into the shower fully clothed. I stayed there for at least 20–30 minutes as bugs continued crawling on me, everything around me moved, the walls melted into themselves, and the voices persisted. I was higher than high and utterly terrified. Despite my state, I had enough sense to realize I was on the verge of a heart attack or stroke. I knew I was flirting with death. It was, by far, the scariest drug experience I'd ever had in my life.

I got out of the shower, soaked from head to toe, and grateful I'd survived. It was a little after 4 p.m. I picked up the pipe and took another hit. I didn't pause again until every iota of crack was gone by Monday morning.

I came down on Monday, and I came down hard. The depression was more real than the bugs that had crawled on me. I called my mom to ask for a plane ticket, cleaned myself up, and headed to the airport. Every television in the airport was broadcasting the same story: Princess Diana had died the day before in a car crash. I left LA and never returned.

Landing back in Reno, I experienced one of my lowest lows. Mom had gotten me a room for the night, but it was now Tuesday morning, and I had to get out by 10 a.m. I was still coming down after smoking for three days straight, alone, with nowhere to go. Worse yet, there weren't any hustles I could perform that early in the morning. I had nothing—literally nothing—except the shirt on my back, pants on my butt, and shoes on my feet. Well, that's not completely correct, because self-pity and deep depression kept me company. I wanted to sleep so badly and would usually have panhandled $1 to get a 93-cent, 32-ounce Natural Ice beer, but even that wasn't productive today. I went to a day shelter and begged for something to eat. They took mercy on me, I managed to get some food, and I passed out.

Mississippi Red Clay

I couldn't seem to silence the voices, and I'd scared Mom. She was incredibly worried about me and decided to send me to a new treatment center called COPAC, located in Brandon, Mississippi, about which she'd heard good things. It was a Caduceus-focused facility, emphasizing and prioritizing treatment for medical staff, nurses, doctors, mental health professionals, and others in similar fields. I didn't belong there among these medical professionals struggling through alcohol, drug, and sex addictions. However, my mom had called in a favor, and she had the money to pay the expensive tuition, which exceeded $25,000.

The program had a 90-day Phase One consisting of intense inpatient treatment. Phase Two, also 90 days, included continued inpatient treatment and offsite work, reintroducing us to working life while providing a stable environment for sobriety. Finally, there was Phase Three, outpatient release, where we learned to sustain ourselves.

The first thing I noticed about Mississippi was the heat. It was May of 1998, and it was hot and humid. The second thing was the culture. Southerners judged your character by the all-important Four F's: Food, Family, Football, and Faith.

- **Food** – The South had the best fried chicken anywhere, hands down. They knew how to

barbecue, and they knew a thing or two about classics like collard greens and cornbread.
- **Family** – Family carried important aspects, such as the legacy of a family name, closeness within families, or dysfunction resulting from its absence.
- **Football** – There were no neutral parties in the South regarding college football. Not having a favorite college football team to root for during bowl season made you akin to a tree falling unheard in the woods.
- **Faith** – God was real, full stop. The only question was which denomination of Christianity you favored—Methodist, AME, Baptist, etc.

Then there was the Mississippi red clay, ever-present just like the yellow jackets and spiders. COPAC was located in Brandon, just outside Jackson, Mississippi, arguably the Blackest city in the United States. Jackson was about 90% Black, and it was my first experience being adjacent to a predominantly Black city. At that time, it seemed the only white people in Jackson were the postmen, the hookers, and the police.

I seriously wanted to remain committed to my sobriety this time. COPAC was a great facility with excellent food and amenities. It provided a different level of treatment because most participants were educated professionals. There were over 100 people in the facility, and I was the only speck of pepper in a sea of salt. However, I'd grown up in white environments, was Ivy League educated, wasn't afraid or bashful, and didn't mind engaging in deep conversations. I blended in well. It also helped that Southerners by nature were very polite, calling me "Mr. Ken" and such. This was, by far, the cleanest facility I'd been in. Things were neat and orderly, which was right up my alley.

Many participants had money, and I'd overhear group discussions about the hierarchy of high-end, celebrity-style treatment centers. Several millionaires and wealthy individuals there had attended facilities like Betty Ford, The Meadows, and Hazelden.

Treatment was going well, with few instances causing me unhappiness. However, two specific situations stood out as uncomfortable. The first was when I signed up for the sex track of therapy. I'd long questioned aspects of my sexuality and past behaviors and figured this would be a good time to address them. I'd already experienced a crack-fueled two-day masturbation marathon, been a male prostitute, and acted as a pimp to underage girls. I needed answers or clarity, which I hoped to find through that group.

Questions & Revelations

It didn't take long for me to realize I didn't have a real sex problem—at least not at the level of my peers in that group. We had to write out our entire sexual history honestly and talk about it in the group. There was a gentleman, a licensed psychiatrist, who frequented gay-friendly parks and had sex five to seven times per night, on average, for weeks at a time. There was the married surgeon who was sleeping with his patients and nurses while on duty. There was a privileged, wealthy young man who'd get jobs at restaurants because he derived sexual gratification from eating food from returning plates or from trash cans. That one was a head-scratcher, because his parents were multimillionaires. In that group, I was introduced to myriad sexual exploits, which made it very clear to me I didn't have a sex problem—at least not at that level.

YES, I'd engaged in gay sex, although I'd never once in my life felt an attraction to a man, but I did that in exchange for some form of survival amenity. The millionaire who ate scraps off strangers' plates and kept getting fired for it did so because that's what provided him with sexual gratification. I never had sex with a man if I wasn't drunk or high, which indicated I was definitely an alcoholic and drug addict, unable to control my behaviors after ingesting chemicals. The well-known psychiatrist who engaged with upwards of fifty random strangers performing oral sex on him for ten days straight demonstrated sexually compulsive behavior. That group helped me understand the difference and was very helpful in my continual life journey. I began analyzing my behaviors from the standpoint of which ones were manageable and which were not.

We each had private and group sessions with counselors. As I pompously strolled one day with that gay, heavyset psychiatrist, he turned to me and said something I found to be the most intensely aggravating, inherently offensive, and napalm-level incendiary statement anyone had ever said to me. He looked at me and said, "Do you know what your problem is, Ken? You have situational ethics. You conveniently choose right or wrong depending on the situation, and because of that, you'll always have problems." He was accusing me of having self-serving morals. For the third time in my life, I had a visceral reaction, and though I didn't throw a punch this time, the string of "fuck yous" and other language I lambasted him with definitely let him know he'd ruffled my feathers.

His words struck me harder than Sam calling me a faggot and pissed me off quicker than having just been spat on. In either of those instances, I had an external entity I could level blame against, but these words, coming from his mouth, were reminiscent of the Mirror on the Wall telling the unbearable truth. Although I hadn't previously been able to name it, I'd spent my entire life surviving, in part, because I was able to morph myself like a chameleon into habitats and environments where people could like me. Even on that day, I knew I still struggled with my identity because life had forced me to adapt in so many ways. Yet, in my naïveté, I thought no one could see through any of my carefully placed facades. I'd convinced myself that I was an amazing actor, an amalgamation of survival skills and life experiences crafted to represent someone greater than I internally knew myself to be. He saw straight through my smoke and mirrors, and quietly but forcefully spoiled the illusion of Kenneth John Horne Turley Miller that had been masterfully toiled over for decades. The fucker saw me, and I instantly hated him for it.

Situational ethics mean having inconsistent integrity or lacking strict, unwavering adherence to an internal code of conduct. My dad had told me about soldiers in WWII who were drafted but refused to pick up a rifle and shoot at another human being. They often became medical personnel or administrative support staff because they weren't necessarily opposed to supporting American interests; they just didn't believe in taking human life. They were called conscientious objectors and were granted immunity from certain roles as a result of their infallible sense of integrity and adherence to their beliefs. If they'd been made to fight as infantrymen, their comrades wouldn't have been able to depend on them in the heat of battle. It seemed the only thing I conscientiously objected to was remaining in or facing my reality, and thus I'd escape whenever it became overwhelming. This psychiatrist, this judge of my character, recognized that I exhibited integrity only when convenient. I was an ethical fraud, and he had the audacity to call me out on it to my face.

The fundamental truth was that he was correct. I'd been lying since I was six years old. I reasoned that I rarely told lies of commission, where I blatantly said, "No, I didn't do that," although I knew I had. However, my lies were usually those of omission, where I conveniently left out incriminating or inconvenient details. He was right about me, but his accuracy didn't quell my anger. Indignant, I went to a counselor to cry and to try to repair the shattered mess I'd instantly become.

When Reasons Feel Justified

I completed Phases I and II, graduated, and then moved out for Phase III. I got an apartment with another program graduate, landed a job at Office Depot, and asked my mom to ship me my car. Just before leaving Reno, during one of my short bouts of legitimate work and sobriety, I had purchased—with her help—a brand-new Subaru Legacy. She was so proud of me and had such empowering faith in me that I knew this was the time. I'd been around other professionals, highly educated and dedicated public servants who were high achievers. We'd spent months bonding, making friendships, and learning how to support each other. I'd even learned to look in that mirror and understand I wasn't a good actor. I had to make real, lasting change. My mom had sacrificed so much, unconditionally sticking with me to get me to this point. She'd literally saved my life.

Back in Reno, there had been a sales competition for Hewlett-Packard printers, with the winner taking home a cash prize. I was a natural salesman, so I decided to take my energy and apply myself. I sold as many printers as I could push, as if they were crack rocks, winning the competition and being crowned the top salesman for the entire West Coast! Things weren't all great, though.

I lasted four days after my car was shipped to me in Brandon before I started tweaking, and five days before I went seeking. It was payday, and I could feel every cell of my body crying out for the drug. My truth was, yes, I wanted to smoke crack—but more important than that was physically possessing the drug. I just needed it in my hand, and that alone would provide some level of comfort, at least enough to dissipate the urge.

There were conversations happening in my head between the part of me that wanted to be an addict and the part that didn't. It was like that story I'd once heard about the two hungry wolves in each man: the one you feed is the one that comes out victorious. One voice spoke to me, reminding me I didn't have to turn left into the drug neighborhood. It would say, "You don't have to do this," or "There's a different way," or "You're a good-looking, intelligent Dartmouth grad—do something with it," or "Call your sponsor." Then, there was the other voice: "Ken, you're a piece of shit. Stop pretending you're not going to use," or "Who are you kidding?", or "You're an Ivy League graduate stuck in Jackson, Mississippi, making $8 an hour—just like those high school kids."

No matter what, one voice always wins. I'd listened to both voices at various points in my life. I'd survived sober for almost three years once, but I'd also smoked crack every fifteen minutes for three days straight. My mom might have thought isolating me from the drug was the greatest deterrent for me. She may have thought that if someone gave me the drug, it would have been the greatest gift. She would have been wrong. The greatest gift any addict can ever receive is a good, justifiable excuse. Addicts just need a reason to justify their use, and relapse is sure to shortly follow. Sometimes—as in my case—the excuse didn't have to be some life-altering emotional event. It could have been as simple as, "Oh well, the traffic at this intersection makes it difficult to turn left."

The two greatest problems with excuses are: (1) they sound legitimate to the person giving them, lending credence to inexcusable behavior; and (2) the first accepted excuse becomes the thread of yarn that unravels the entire garment.

Eventually, Mom's love and a good-paying job be damned, I turned left. Why? I was an addict. I still hated myself. That was the only excuse I needed: that I was not worthy of the joys and serenity of being clean. I entered into a new world in Jackson, Mississippi. I needed to explore my bottom more. One little excuse facilitated the life of the next, each excuse begetting another, dividing like cells in a petri dish until they took on a complete life of their own. What had once been a knitted sweater was now just a ball of yarn, stained with Mississippi red clay.

On Addiction

I saw a young man who looked like he sold drugs, likely fourteen or fifteen years old, riding a bike, and motioned to him. He came over, and after our ceremonial "you lookin'?" and "what you got?" drug communication, he assured me he could get me what I needed but wanted to get in the car. Police monitored the streets, and he didn't want to do an exchange openly. He leaned his bike against a pole and entered on the passenger side. I explained I wanted $100 of crack. He then pulled out a gun and robbed me. I had $400 on me but gave him only the $100. By that point, I really wanted dope and didn't want to give him all my money. He got back on his bike and rode away. I thought about speeding up and running him over, but in the end, I just wanted to get high and went looking elsewhere.

I found another person who escorted me to a shotgun house. In Mississippi, these homes were built so that when you opened the front door, there was a long hallway leading directly to the back door. If a person fired a shotgun from either side, they'd just hit the other door. Standing at the front door and facing the back, the left side had three bedrooms, and the right side had two bedrooms, a communal kitchen, and a bathroom. Every bedroom in that rooming house had a crack smoker as an occupant. A nice-looking older Black prostitute lived in the first room, and an older gentleman who worked catch-out day-labor jobs occupied the second. The third room had a white prostitute and her light-skinned gorilla pimp. Each room in this degenerate and decrepit house was occupied by people I shouldn't have been around. I needed to use the bathroom. I turned on the light, and hundreds of roaches scattered. I would get to know this bathroom well over the next six months. There was a tub and shower, but no running hot water, and the shower didn't work. I befriended the Black prostitute first, then the seventy-year-old man, and both became people I hung out with. I was this crazy, light-skinned, educated, proper-talking guy from the West Coast, and they were the simple-living, never-left-Jackson local residents I became crack friends with.

There are different types of communities in America, ranging from project housing units to suburbs to upscale gated communities. In '98, I found myself in a hood—a place where 100% of residents were local, tourists didn't visit, and inner-city Black Jackson, Mississippi, had its own rules. There were places I knew were inherently bad or risky, and other places heavily monitored by police, so they were avoided. People grew up together here on the lower socioeconomic scale, and there were existing hierarchies within that society. There was a common familiarity in the hood among locals, which made it easier to detect when something was awry.

A Curious & Hard World

I lost my job at Office Depot and started working in a traditional Southern crack house. It was my second stint operating as a team member in a crack house, but this one was more organized—professional, if you will. It was an easy transition because it was next door to the rooming house where I had relapsed. Everyone associated with the crack house had a job and a place, layered for security and efficiency purposes. First, you had one or two "Post-ups" outside the house looking for police activity, ready to give the signal if danger came rolling through. If a familiar client approached, they would knock on the house's single door, and the "Doorman" would acknowledge only a knock from a Post-up, unlocking and opening the door to the first room, which was the kitchen. The Doorman stayed vigilant, stationed behind a door reinforced with two-by-fours nailed to the floor and propped against the door to stall any occasional police bust attempts. The money then moved from the client to the Doorman. The next station was in the living room, where the Runner was positioned, collecting money and passing it along to the Dealer, who was usually stationed behind a locked bedroom door. The working girls stayed tucked in the room with the Dealer or in the living room, ready to turn tricks or help hide evidence, whichever way the door swung. The Dealer was king. The hierarchy was clear: Post-up, Doorman, Runner, Dealer.

If you came to the house with $200–$300 and wanted a girl, you'd break off a piece for the house crew, and the Dealer would assign you a room and a girl—or girls. Amid the burnt-plastic chemical smell of crack and the bass of loud, usually blues music thumping from the speakers, there was a constant cloud of cigarette smoke blended with the dull undertone of hot sweat and sex. It was an element alive in its own right, an ambiance familiar to those living the life. There were no time clocks to punch in and out, yet we all knew when to show up. We were located about a block from a school, and everyone knew distributing drugs while school was in session resulted in double or triple jail time, so we didn't operate during school hours. No exceptions. From 7:30 a.m. to 4 p.m., we rested and prepared for the night. The house was our job site, not our resting place. There were no written job descriptions, but the roles, tasks, and expectations of every worker rivaled those of the finest high-end consultancy. It worked, so we kept doing it.

It wasn't all work. On lighter nights, we'd party together. The lights in the front of the house would go off, signaling to locals we were closed for business. Larry, our dealer, would offer up rocks to each of us. Looking back, it was like the happy hour of the street world. His team would come together, celebrating our hard work and success. Like a diamond appraiser offering his most precious inventory, Larry would spread out crack rocks of various sizes on a large tray, neatly arranged. When you're in the game, they might as well have been diamonds. They looked beautiful. According to the hierarchy, we'd choose our rock, and without explicit command, we knew the appropriate size for our station. Women, always lowest on the totem pole, went last. Though I liked my Natural Ice beer, Larry and many other Southerners favored Seagram's Extra Dry Gin. I once bought him a full case, and it was gone in just three days. This was how we lived day to day, week to week, confined to that ever-shrinking world that perpetually distanced us from any meaningful existence some had once known.

It was a curious and hard world. Yet, as all shells have an underbelly, there was also a softer side to things I witnessed in that life. Larry kept a girl by his side for nearly ten years. She was his Top Girl, the queen atop the hierarchy of women. In her prime, she was a moneymaker for him, not only turning tricks but also keeping the working-girl workforce ready and in line. She was a recruiter, quality control manager, comptroller, executive assistant, and department supervisor—in corporate terms. Hierarchy exists everywhere, even among working girls, and her position as Vice President of Operations, Services Division, meant she answered only to Larry. By the time I entered the operation, street life had caught up with her, and she was dying.

Visibly and by all accounts, there was no missing it. She was deteriorating and awaiting death. But she would lie all day in Larry's bed, and he would let her stay there with no expectations of work or responsibility. He was old-school, real Southern; a fair man who treated us well, even in our addiction. Maybe he loved her—maybe it was an expression or version of love that only exists in that drug-fueled microcosm. She had a weekly regular she would still service, even in this holding pattern for death; six years with this same customer. Facing impending death, he'd become her only customer. I'm sure the mark had seen the evidence of her life eroding month after month. Yet, though he could have picked any other prostitute, he kept his weekly appointment with her. Perhaps he loved her as well. In a beautifully twisted way, he provided meaning to her continued existence; a modicum of worth for still "providing" for her man.

After taking a few hours to get ready—"putting her uniform on," as we'd call it—she'd go out and turn her trick. Usually within the hour, she was back. She'd give Larry all the money she earned, remove her uniform, and crawl into bed to await death or her next weekly standing appointment. Pimping is a business that can afford at best few redundancies and even less dead weight. Underperformers were punished, retrained, and/or replaced. Yet here they were, ten years into their routine. That was her world: drugs, tricks, and bed to await death. At this stage, she could barely earn enough money to warrant being a part of the house. She knew it, Larry knew it, we all knew it. Yet he kept her at his side. The dynamics of human relationships, especially between men and women, leave great, unsolved mysteries. What Larry saw in her that prompted that unwavering and loyal commitment of "till death do us part," I'll never fully know. However, I recognized then—and now—it was a beautiful reminder of humanity. Perhaps it was duty, or the remnant of a love forged before the "life." But the conduct of the Larrys of the world imprinted upon me a certain dignity and respect I would carry with me in working with the women in that life.

I worked my way up the hierarchy, eventually becoming Larry's number two. He liked my intelligence and gave me the additional duty of overseeing the girls, becoming his right hand. He considered wrangling the girls a general pain in the ass anyway, so he was happy to pass them off. I was happy to have a steady supply of dope. Sometimes I'd have to deal with the Johns, but most times I did simple things like taking the girls shopping so they could get feminine products. I also kept the girls in line. Larry once rented multiple rooms in a motel and brought four of his girls to service customers. He operated in one room, and I in another. I set some rules for the girls, which were simple:

- Don't touch my money.
- Don't touch my dope.
- Don't answer the door without permission.
- Don't answer the phone without permission.

They were incredibly simple rules to follow, but not two minutes after I laid down the law, the phone rang, and Shannon, one of Larry's white girls, answered it.

"Bitch, didn't I just say—?" was about all I got out of my mouth before I slapped her on the ass like a petulant child. She recoiled in shock and began crying. I snatched the phone from her—it was Larry calling from next door. He asked what was happening, and she began trying to explain herself. I told him the rules I'd just set and what she'd done, so he asked her to get back on the phone, then berated her, telling her I could do whatever I needed to do to keep them in line. It was the only time I ever laid hands on a woman, but I gained that respect from her and the other girls.

I did whatever was necessary, within reason, to keep the girls happy. For instance, Larry's crack house had running hot water but no tub. There were a total of six girls—three white and three Black—and they all liked to bathe. So, I'd get a bucket, fill it with hot water at Larry's, then go fill the tub in the rooming house next door for them to use. Another task was to help keep the peace between them. They operated in harmony most days, but flare-ups happened every now and then. It was better for me to handle it because Larry, though a very nice guy and not a gorilla, was an ordered businessman, and they all knew it. He preferred things to happen a certain way and knew balance needed to be maintained.

One day, one of the girls violated a rule by attempting to catch a date in front of the crack house. Shannon was drunk—but that was no excuse—and she knew better. The alcohol must have blocked her judgment. It was strictly forbidden to operate within three blocks of the house, so as not to bring unwanted visibility or possible exposure to the police. But rules, especially in this unforgiving world, were broken at a cost she couldn't yet imagine.

CHAPTER 8: MY REFLECTIONS

The most dangerous thing an addict can have isn't a dealer—it's a good excuse. The moment I convinced myself that my pain justified a relapse, the battle was already lost. And the thing about excuses is, they multiply. Once you allow one, the next becomes easier. Before you know it, you've rewritten reality to make it seem like you never had a choice.

1. **Love, Obligation, and the Weight of Expectations** - Sometimes, we mistake obligation for love, stability for happiness, and convenience for commitment. I wanted to be a father, a husband, a provider—not just because it was the right thing to do, but because I needed an anchor. I thought if I stepped into a new role, if I played the part well enough, it would fix me. But roles don't heal wounds. Titles don't replace love. And a marriage built on need instead of desire is just another kind of prison.
2. **Rejection Is a Dangerous Trigger** - A single moment of rejection can undo years of progress. I thought my sobriety was strong because I had purpose. But purpose without connection is hollow, and when my wife pushed me away, it

cracked something deep inside. Addiction doesn't need much of an opening. A whisper of self-doubt, a moment of loneliness, a story you tell yourself about not being wanted—it's enough to light the fuse. I walked out that door looking for an escape, and I found it.

3. **Falling Feels Like Flying—Until You Hit the Ground** - At first, every relapse feels like freedom. The weight of rejection, failure, and expectation disappears. You tell yourself this is what you needed, that you deserve this, that you're finally in control. But it's all a lie. The fall feels good—until you realize the ground is rushing up to meet you, and this time, you might not get back up.
4. **Survival Can Become a Trap** - I learned how to survive at any cost. Whether it was hustling, working in the crack house, or managing the women, I adapted. But survival isn't the same as living. The more I played the game, the more it consumed me. The deeper I went, the harder it became to remember who I had been before. And when you spend enough time in the dark, you start to believe the light was never real.
5. **The Mirror Never Lies** - That psychiatrist saw straight through me, and I hated him for it. I built my life around playing whatever role the moment required, shifting my ethics to fit the situation, justifying every choice with whichever excuse was most convenient. But the truth was simple: I was

running—running from responsibility, from love, from rejection, from myself. Until I stopped running, nothing would ever change.

6. **The Choice Was Always Mine** - Every relapse, every mistake, every descent into addiction—I told myself it was inevitable. But that was just another lie. The truth is, I always had a choice. The hardest part of recovery isn't quitting drugs, alcohol, or the lifestyle—it's accepting responsibility for every choice that led you there. The question isn't whether you can change; it's whether you're finally ready to stop making excuses.

CHAPTER 9
THE BREAKING POINT

I was notified by a doorman that Shannon was strolling right outside the house, but Larry also overheard. Larry's response was simple: "Bring that bitch back!" I immediately went out and said, "Shannon, you know you're not supposed to be out here," and it was like it awakened her from her drunken stupor. She was my favorite girl—a beautiful, petite white girl from a sexually abusive past who was a complete alcoholic. I realized she was just drunk, and I felt bad for her. She had explained to me before that sometimes, when out partying, she'd be so drunk that when she came to, there would be some random stranger on top of her. She began crying as I escorted her back across the street; we both knew what was coming. She knew she'd messed up and there was a price to pay. Still, like a chastened child awaiting punishment, she entered the house and reported to Larry to bear the consequences of her rule-breaking.

I decided to try my hand once again at sobriety. I joined

an inpatient treatment center in the Jackson area. It was a definite downgrade from COPAC, and I was back among street-level addicts who were also trying to gain control over themselves and their lives. Most were there voluntarily, but some were court-appointed or otherwise mandated. There were crack-addicted women trying to regain custody or visitation rights to their children. I remember becoming incredulous at a woman who'd repeatedly left her children to turn tricks and get high, repeating the cycle until she finally went home. The grandparents had come over to visit and found the young kids alone, hungry, dirty, and without the slightest clue where their mom was, so they took them. Sitting in these groups, listening to these stories, my heart would break, but there was also the reality that this woman was in no condition to care for her children. Until she learned how to truly implement a program that altered her behavior—and until she learned to love mothering in sobriety more than she feared someone taking away her kids due to drug use—she wouldn't be ready to parent.

Forwarded Mail

This treatment center was different from any other I'd attended. We sat in groups on overturned five-gallon buckets and shared our stories. It was almost as if they wanted us to be uncomfortable with the environment, so we'd desire never to return. It was obvious they had no idea what living in a crack environment was really like, because this was still a drastic upgrade. I was clean, showered, fed, stable, not fearing the police or a stick-up crew. I had all my clothing and belongings with me, including my suits and the items I'd collected from the good jobs I'd held while in Jackson.

One day, I received some forwarded letters in the mail from my mom. One envelope contained a credit card and said I could withdraw $500 cash. Seeing that, I started tweaking immediately. All I had to do was call the number on the card, and the cash would be transferred to me—my fingers about caught fire dialing the phone. However, they informed me I'd have to wait a day before I could access the cash. Another envelope contained a letter from the corporate team at Office Depot regarding the Hewlett-Packard printer competition I'd won, informing me I'd been awarded $3,000. That night, I climbed over the fence and escaped the treatment center.

I got the cash the next day and went back to Larry's. Upon returning, I found out that while I was in treatment, the police had raided the place. They'd tried to break down the door, but the 2x4s did their job. Larry had managed to stash his cash and the drugs from the safe before they were able to get in. The police had messed up because they raided during the day, which was our off-time, and no activities were happening. Larry had already been arrested and released during the month I was in treatment.

I soon received the $3,000, and I told Larry I wanted to buy quite a bit of dope. I looked at Shannon, motioned, and off to one of the rooms we went.

Spiraling Out of Control

I had a great time with her, then wanted some beer. I went next door to the older Black prostitute in room one, kicked it with her for a bit, then went to the older man's room. He was out working, but I went inside and hid $1,000 cash. Afterward, I left and walked to the corner store, passing a man about my age as I entered. I bought about eight 40oz beers—as much as I could hold—and asked the other guy if he smoked crack. He acknowledged that he did, and I offered to smoke with him from my stash back at the rooming house. We headed back with the beer. Returning to the old man's room, I set the beer and rocks on the table, then lit up. We were smoking and joking when Larry summoned me. I went next door; he just wanted something menial. When I returned, reality hit me—my dope was gone. The guy had stolen it and run off. I asked around to see if anyone had noticed which way he went, but I was still the outsider in their world. They'd grown up together, knew each other's kinfolk, and this was their neighborhood.

I was beyond pissed. I ran back over to Larry and told him I needed his gun. He asked what for, and I told him how the dude had just ripped me off for seven rocks. He looked at me with a face I'd never seen before and said, "Motherfucker, are you crazy?" He then lit into me as if I were Shannon caught breaking rules, cursing me out and reminding me I wasn't from around these parts. He warned me that I couldn't just run down the street with a shotgun looking to shoot someone who stole a few rocks. It wouldn't take long before the guy, his people, his family, or the police had me lying in a pool of blood, left pondering just how stupid I'd been as the light faded. I didn't even know the guy's name. At that moment, I had a profound epiphany: this was Jackson, and I was the "mark." I was just a Subaru-driving, fancy-talking, Dartmouth-educated West Coaster looking for a good time—no different from the California "marks" who would come to Reno for weekend parties. Technically, I wasn't even a Subaru driver anymore since, within days of relapsing, I'd given a friend $50 and my car keys to buy dope and beer. He panicked when a police car got behind him, sped off, crashed into another vehicle, and fled the scene at crackhead speed. The police never contacted me, and I never saw my brand-new, less-than-a-year-old car again. I went through the $3,000 in three days. Frustrated, depressed, and spent, I left Mississippi.

A Tough Detox

I returned to Reno, went to detox again, and then entered the county's 28-day treatment program. There, I met this green-eyed, pale-skinned, alternative-looking girl named Danielle. Her street name was Turtle, and we started talking. Things got serious between us quickly, and her graduation date was approaching. She was leaving three days before me and offered for me to come stay with her once I got out. We figured we could help keep each other clean because she wasn't into crack, and I wasn't into her drug of choice—the speedball. She loved to inject a mixture of heroin and cocaine. Our conversations revealed she was genuinely a good person. She'd been prostituting since she was a teen, traveled coast to coast, and was far more streetwise than I was. Three days after her release, she picked me up and took me to her house in Sparks, Nevada, the next town over from Reno. Her dad owned many investment properties and allowed her to stay in this one for free.

The first thing she asked me to do was remove all of her rigs—her needles—that she'd stashed around the house. I found 23 on the first day and a few more later. We were determined to remain sober and change our lives. We attended meetings together, kept each other accountable, and existed peacefully as lovers, listening to artists ranging from Kenny Lattimore to Sisters of Mercy. We both found jobs—I did catch-out jobs and temp agency work, and she did administrative tasks for her dad's real estate business.

I would get off at 4:30 pm and wait for her to pick me up from my temp job at a warehouse. One day, she was late. 4:30 pm came and went, followed by 5:30 pm, then 6:30 pm. Her house was only about five miles from this job, and I considered walking home but decided to keep waiting in the hot sun. Just after 7 pm, she pulled up, glassy-eyed and obviously high. I'd never been around a speedballer, but I'd been around addicts and alcoholics since I was six, and I knew the look. I was pissed and asked where she'd been, though I already knew. She drove, looking straight ahead, and said, "I relapsed."

Fuck. Fuck. Fuck. It's all I could say, because I knew—beyond any shadow of a doubt—I knew this violated a universal law in the Rooms of Recovery. It's simply and undeniably this: If you are having sex with someone who is actively using drugs, you're fucked. Sure, there are politically correct ways to phrase it, but addiction doesn't care about sensitive ears. One hundred percent of the time, without fail, if you're in a relationship with—let alone having sex with—someone who is actively using, you're done. You will relapse. Treatment is a waste of time, and I knew it. I really liked Danielle and knew that, outside the addiction, she was an amazing human. I was 40 days clean, and she'd made it to 43. I followed my girl and relapsed.

We were addicts. We started doing crack together because it was the more affordable way to change our perceptions of reality. I was a 38-year-old man, panhandling and hustling any way I could to support our habit. We had a very nice three-bedroom house for free, and our place became a hangout spot for addicts and dope dealers. We'd throw parties, and at one such party, two 15- or 16-year-old lesbians approached us for some crack. We sold it to them, and they disappeared into a room together. They came back high and wanting more crack, asking if there was anything they could do to get more since they didn't have any money left. I immediately offered to get them dates. They were sitting in an oversized La-Z-Boy chair when they looked at me—one sitting on the other's lap—and said, "We won't do a guy, but will they pay to watch us do each other?" It was a question that froze me in time. I thought to myself, “What are you doing? You have two 15-year-old white girls, high on crack that you sold them, and you’re contemplating finding dates. What the hell are you going to do when they go back to school tomorrow and tell on you?” Even in my addiction, I knew better this time and walked away.

The insanity increased as our addiction did. While at work, Danielle stole a check from her dad, and we tried to cash it. It was made out for $23,000—obviously a real estate payment for some transaction—and we desperately searched for a place that would cash it for us. No matter how hard we tried, no one would honor the check. Her dad found out and went ballistic. He quickly kicked us out, and we ended up back on the streets. I hustled for a room at the Fireside Inn Motel, sharing it with another user named Mike. My main hustle was running for the D-boys. I was drinking and did something stupid, which pissed Danielle off. I ended up in jail on a misdemeanor, and Danielle went back on the stroll. I was in for just a few days. After I got out, I asked around to see if anyone had seen Turtle and found out she’d connected with a gorilla pimp named JC. I discovered where they were holed up, fueled myself up on beer, strapped on my Captain Save-A-Hoe cape, and went off to Danielle’s rescue.

A Rock & A Hard Place

I found them in an area of Reno that I knew of but was unfamiliar with. The primary drug used in that area was heroin, and it was a different world than my crack world. In my world, our motel use was mostly transitory, and my grandest goal at the time was always to get a room for a week. That was a jackpot for me. In their heroin world, they were able to secure rooms for a month or longer. They dealt with different dealers from other areas of the country who specialized in heroin, not crack. These two different drug worlds could coexist as long as territories were respected. With that knowledge, I went to the motel where I knew they were. I knocked, and a large, dark-skinned, genuinely gorilla-looking dude opened the door and asked, "What's up?" I asked if Danielle was in there, and he asked who I was. I replied, "Don't worry about who the fuck I am. Is Danielle in there?" Before he could respond, she heard me and came to the door. I ignored him completely and told her, "Get your shit and let's go." The pimp was pissed, so I invited him to step outside, not wanting to disrespect the room or fight inside where he might have weapons or other people. I was more than willing to fight for my woman.

It was a few days before Memorial Day in 2000. Danielle loved me and was happy to have escaped the gorilla. We started dreaming together of getting clean again as we walked back toward the Fireside Inn Motel. We arrived at my third-floor room and, before entering, I turned to her and asked her to do me a favor. She said sure, and that's when I told her I had a date for her. Like Siri before her, she gave me a disgusted look, disappointed that I would ask that of her. She wondered if I'd picked her up just to put her back on the stroll. She quietly said "OK"—an "OK" filled with resolve, recognizing that I wasn't different, and that no one loved her. She was a prostitute, a representation of value exchanged for something else of perceived worth. It was an "OK" acknowledging she was simply a breathing representation of the inanimate dollar bills she'd soon bring back to me.

She left and turned the trick. Upon returning, she entered our two-bed room, removed some clothing, and lay down with me. She was still angry, and we began to argue—perhaps over the temperature of the room, the color of the sky, or the going rate for rooibos tea. I'd hurt her, and she wanted me to know it. Wearing her bra and panties, she got her sexy ass out of my bed and plopped down onto Mike's bed. Mike looked at me as if to say, "It's not my fault," but I didn't care. I felt disrespected and began fuming. Some other people we knew entered the room, and she didn't bother getting dressed or covering herself. One of the guys started chopping at me, cracking jokes and talking out of the side of his neck. No matter how forcefully I explained that I wasn't in the mood, he kept going. Eventually, I asked him to step outside and have a smoke with me. Once outside, I grabbed him and soon had him hanging over the balcony. I might have let him go, but the other guys from the room grabbed both of us, pulling him back over the railing. Although the room was partially mine, I'd disrespected it, and Mike demanded I leave to cool off.

The look on Danielle's face as I walked away from that room—her reclining on the bed in her underwear with my friend, our stupid argument over nothing, and my general status in life—all spun around in my head. I had an idea. I began walking.

I soon found myself at my mom's house. I had a key to her place and a standing offer to return—but only if I was clean and sober. I opened the door, looked around, and burglarized my mom's house. I stole her jewelry, two checks from her checkbook, and some sleeping pills. Returning downtown, I cashed the checks, got a room at the Sage Motel, and got incredibly high. I hit the lowest point I'd ever reached in my life. I sat and cried, remembering how many times I'd reached out to my mom over the years. She'd always say, "Kenneth, meet me at this Denny's," and proceed to check on me and make sure I had a proper meal. I reflected on how she'd literally spent the last 20 years—since I was 18—paying for my treatment in various centers, each time hoping it would stick.

I thought about how, at both of her near-death experiences—Sam shooting her and her suicide attempt—I'd shown no emotion. I was emotionally unavailable and incapable of even a simple response like tears when watching the only person who had ever loved me unconditionally struggle to stay alive. She'd shared with me that it was the combination of Sam, Dennis, and my treatment of her that caused her to want to end her pain, but I knew—I freaking knew—it was her disappointment in me that had crushed her heart the most. I now knew the look. I'd seen it on her face in the hospital but hadn't fully comprehended it then. Janice, Lora, Chrissy, Siri, Stephanie, and Danielle had now helped me fully understand just how cold and hurtful I, or my behaviors, could be. Situational ethics. I had ethics until I wanted or needed alcohol or drugs.

Overburdened with guilt, I called my mom. I didn't know what else to do and had never felt as disappointed in myself as I did at that moment. I didn't know how, but I needed to try and fix it. I heard her soft voice say, "Kenneth, I cannot believe you did this to me." She already knew it was me who had burglarized her. She had called the police and let me know there was a warrant out for my arrest. For the second time that day, I'd completely betrayed the trust of a woman I loved, and her disappointment in me was palpable. I had tried so many treatment centers, churches, and programs, yet I could not see a way for the pain to end. The worst memory ever popped into my head, and I reflected on how many times I'd thought about killing my mom—literally ending her life by various means—so I could receive my inheritance and buy more dope. It felt like Dave Grohl was playing drums in my heart as I swallowed every sleeping pill I'd stolen, resolving that I didn't deserve to wake up. I'd now done the worst thing I'd ever done in my life, and felt I had one last act to perform. Stomach full of sleeping pills, waiting for them to finally allow me peace, I walked to the small downtown police station and turned myself in for burglarizing my mom. I felt it was only fitting that I should die while awaiting jail. Another hurt soul's disappointed voice joined the others: "If I had died yesterday, it wouldn't have been soon enough." Poignant. Pithy. True.

Regret & Remorse

I didn't want to hurt another soul. I now understood that sometimes it was, in fact, better for some people to kill themselves.

On the way to the police station, a different thought whispered its way into my mind. It was an acknowledgment that I didn't want to die—I just wanted the pain I caused and the pain I felt to stop. I realized I should not desire to die simply because I hadn't yet learned how to live.

I was arrested, and the intake officer asked me to urinate in a cup. I agreed. After providing the sample, I told him I'd taken sleeping pills.

I was unceremoniously whisked away to Washoe Med, where they handcuffed me to a gurney and had me swallow charcoal. It didn't take long before it felt like charcoal was pouring out of every hole I had. Whatever substances were inside began expelling from me, and fast. I didn't know if I wanted to vomit, have diarrhea, or both simultaneously—but to say it was a shit show is an understatement.

I was arraigned soon after and charged with burglary and internal possession of a controlled substance. I jokingly called the latter charge "walking while high." Later, the burglary charge was dropped because my mom refused to give a statement or testify. She knew it would be my second felony burglary, sending me away for years. Once again, my mom had saved my life. I knew I didn't deserve her.

Internal possession was a charge that allowed Nevada police to arrest people for having drugs in their bloodstream.

It was another felony, carrying a potential prison sentence of up to three years. I appeared before Judge Peter Breen in Drug Court, where addicts could have their sentences reduced or removed if they successfully completed a year-long treatment program. I was sentenced to the year-long program at Center Street Mission, beginning with a 30-day complete lockdown.

Looking For Work

After the Phase I lockdown, we began receiving day passes to look for work. As I went out, I'd occasionally see Danielle on the streets, but I knew to avoid any meaningful relationship if I hoped to stay sober. The program was effective, but it seemed to hit the same snag with me—they were Christian-based. I believed God had saved my life: when I took those sleeping pills, when I stood in that cold shower after overdosing, and when I wanted to jump off the bridge before that. I'd become agnostic, acknowledging a God or higher being capable of altering my behavior and holding me accountable, but I didn't associate that energy with any specific religion. I'd tried Christian programs before, and even a Muslim-run program while in prison. I was spiritual but not religious. Though my intelligence and love of reading allowed me to preach with the best of them, I felt like a Christian impostor aided by intellect. As demonstrated throughout history, a man who can learn the Bible—or any religious text, for that matter—can become a danger unto himself, let alone the public. I didn't want another strike against my situational ethics.

Again, I used the Chinese method: taking the lessons I wanted from this treatment and leaving the rest.

I befriended a young, 21-year-old Hispanic guy in treatment, who invited me to live with him. He had committed a low-level drug crime and was also sentenced by the Drug Court, though he wasn't an addict. He had a mother-in-law setup with a camper on his property, plus space in the attic, so I moved in. I eventually found another job, as required by the program. A little over a week after moving in, I got paid. Before the ink on the check dried, I relapsed and began drinking again. Unable to control my drinking, I started experiencing blackout episodes but continued attending treatments at Center Street.

During one blackout, I began talking to a teenage girl who lived in the house. While drunk, I wondered aloud why her breasts hadn't developed yet and asked her to show me her flat chest. All jokes stopped as she became upset by my comments. She told her mom what I'd asked her to do, resulting in my friend kicking me out.

I caught a lucky break after the incident. I was able to inform the counselors I was struggling with the religious aspect of the treatment, feeling it hindered my recovery. Though I'd slipped up, I assured the Drug Court I remained committed to sobriety. They transferred me to a 30-day inpatient treatment program in Elko, Nevada, a state-run facility. However, they made it clear that relapse was a violation of probation and that Elko was my last chance before being sent to prison.

Elko was located in the high desert and stood out to me

because there were many young teenage girls in this co-ed facility alongside grown men, a few of us former pimps. Those young women—all of them—were acutely aware of themselves and their sexuality, which made it even more confusing that the state had intermixed us.

Stories In Treatment

On the evening of my first day in Elko, I sat in the smoking area to begin mingling with people. I didn't smoke, but I was very sociable. One of the girls approached and sat next to me. She was a decent-looking blonde but seemed like a butch lesbian. She appeared to be between 17 and 21, which made her stand out among the younger teenage girls. I was intrigued because, unlike the younger girls, she didn't seem very interested in looking fast or desirable. I asked her what her story was, and she lit a cigarette.

She began by telling me she was a pimp and that she was 18. I chuckled in disbelief, but she gave me a look that showed she was serious. She pointed to every girl in the facility, calling out their ages as she went. They were all between 14 and 18 years old. Many of them were working girls or teenage runaways on the path to walking the streets. One or two were drug addicts whose parents sent them to the treatment center in hopes of scaring them straight or correcting their behavior. I'll never understand the logic of parents sending their young children to a treatment center among seasoned and manipulative addicts, streetwalkers, and drug dealers, hoping they'll somehow get better.

My new friend said that while in Las Vegas, she had picked up a trick for one of her teenage girls. As her girl and the guy were in the backseat having sex, he decided he wanted anal. Her girl reminded him that he hadn't paid for that, and my friend warned the trick. The guy told her to "Shut up, bitch, and mind your fucking business," so she explained—or rather, demonstrated—exactly how she managed her business's assets. She pulled out a gun, and the guy bolted from the car. She stepped out and fired a single shot, striking him in the ass, then sped off. She'd "literally busted a cap in his ass," she mused, and we both fell out laughing. In court, she and the girl concocted a believable enough story that landed her in Drug Court instead of prison.

She shared many other stories, and we became friends. We talked about my observation of her hair-trigger temper and her dislike for women. She was a gorilla pimp who, even at 18 years old, saw other women as commodities—a vulnerable, controllable means to an end.

I also met a young Black man who told the story of his relapse and how he ended up in treatment. He was in his 20s and absolutely handsome; a better-looking model than I'd ever been. He and his fiancée were headed to a couples' vacation in Hawaii. The night before the trip, he decided to visit an adult store to get some toys for the vacation. While there, he visited one of the small booths where adult movies played. These rooms were meant for just one individual, so small that you could touch the walls on both sides without fully outstretching your arms. He was a meth addict and began a cycle of smoking and masturbating. The movies were activated by quarters, and it was possible to pay extra to have a live girl dance behind a protective screen. In his meth-fueled addiction, he masturbated and remained stuck in this little room for three whole days, stopping only to get more quarters. He'd beaten my two-day, crack-fueled record—but that's meth for you. To save his relationship, he submitted to his girlfriend's demands that he go through treatment again. He still owed her a trip to Hawaii.

Committed To Sobriety

Stories like these were common in treatment. Every person I encountered had tales of believing they had control over their drug use, only to discover through some event that their drugs controlled them. Each of us had suffered by hurting others and ourselves—sometimes involving people who cared about us, and other times involving complete strangers. Unfortunately, my pimp friend's anger got the best of her one day, and she was kicked out of the program just one week shy of graduation. As for my model-looking friend, his fiancée had unwittingly placed her beautiful lover in a facility filled with women who openly discussed the things they wanted to do to him. Women—not men—warned him not to get caught slipping with one of the other clients in a quiet corner or by a utility closet.

After the Elko treatment, I was more committed than ever to remaining sober. I genuinely wanted it this time. I was working the night shift and living in the Mandala House, a halfway house that helped residents transition back into normal life. On my 45th day of sobriety—and my third day at Mandala House—a fellow worker approached me and said someone was looking for me. I initially brushed him off, but he insisted the guy really needed to talk with me. I went out to meet him and discovered he was a sheriff's deputy there to arrest me for a misdemeanor offense. Shocked, I asked what I'd done and was informed that I was being arrested for "Annoying a Minor."

I was booked again at Parr Blvd., but it wasn't until I saw the charging documents that I understood what was happening. According to those documents, I'd said, "Show me your breasts," to a teenager while I was drunk and staying in my Drug Court buddy's mother-in-law's camper. Charges had been filed, and Nevada had a law making it illegal to "annoy a minor," classifying it as a misdemeanor. I was beside myself—I couldn't believe I'd been arrested merely for words. I vaguely remembered standing by the refrigerator and making some remark about the girl's flat chest, but I never touched her or made threats. She got upset, and I remembered walking out of the house. Unfortunately, I couldn't recall more details. I was sentenced and served 30 days. Shortly thereafter, I relapsed.

I appeared in Drug Court again. This relapse was my third strike, and they'd had enough. The judge was done issuing chances for me to squander, so he sent me to prison for the first time, for the crime of Internal Possession of a Controlled Substance.

Incarceration is the state of being confined or imprisoned, typically as a result of a criminal conviction or sanction. A person can serve their time in a drug treatment center, mental health facility, jail, or prison. Each facility has varying degrees of severity depending on the crime committed and the individual involved. People often confuse jail and prison, using the terms interchangeably as "locked up." However, while a person undergoing incarceration or "serving time" can do so in either jail or prison, the environments differ significantly.

CHAPTER 9: MY REFLECTIONS

I thought I had hit rock bottom before. But my real rock bottom wasn't the missions, detoxes, jail cells, or streets. It wasn't the prostitution, pimping, or hustling. It wasn't even the suicidal thoughts. It was realizing I'd become a man I would have once despised—a man who could justify anything if it meant getting high. My ethics had become paper-thin, situational, and flexible enough to let me sleep at night, regardless of my actions.

1. **Addiction Doesn't Care About Promises** - Danielle and I thought we could save each other. But addiction doesn't work that way. It doesn't negotiate or compromise, and it certainly doesn't allow love to overpower its pull. One relapse was all it took. She went first; I followed. Within days, we weren't two people trying to stay clean—we were two addicts sinking together. Love and logic stood no chance against the weight of our habits.
2. **The Moment You Know You're Lost** - There are moments in addiction when you suddenly see yourself from the outside, moments when the fog lifts just enough to realize how far you've fallen. That was me, sitting before two teenage girls high

on crack, considering finding them customers. That was me, trying to cash a stolen $23,000 check with Danielle, believing it would solve everything. That was me, breaking into my own mother's home and stealing from the only person who ever truly loved me. In those moments, you don't just lose control—you lose yourself.

3. **When Even the Streets Push You Away** - I had traveled down dark paths before, but Reno brought me to my lowest point. By the time I found myself in that motel with Danielle, my mind was shattered. It wasn't merely addiction anymore—it was despair. It was waking up and realizing that the game had consumed me entirely. It was the shame of seeing my mother's face in my head, knowing I'd betrayed her, knowing that her disappointment in me ran deeper than any wound she'd ever suffered from others. It was understanding, in a way I never had before, that the problem wasn't just the drugs—it was me.
4. **A Moment of Clarity Isn't Enough** - There was a moment—standing at the police station, confessing to burglarizing my mother's home, waiting for the sleeping pills to take effect—when I realized I didn't truly want to die. I just didn't know how to live. But realization isn't enough. Clarity isn't enough. Wanting to change isn't enough. Because the moment you believe you've figured it

out, addiction reminds you just how easy it is to slip back.

5. **Prison Wasn't the End—It Was a Mirror** - I thought prison would be my end, but really, it was just another mirror. Another version of the same life I'd been living—rules, hierarchy, survival. Another chance to either face who I was or keep running. By then, I knew one thing for certain: I was tired of running. The real question was—was I strong enough to finally stop?

PART FOUR
LOCKED UP TO WAKE UP

CHAPTER 10
PRISION SENTENCES

I arrived at the Washoe County Jail on Parr Boulevard in Reno, and nothing about the place suggested comfort. It was run by the county, managed by the sheriff's department, and served as a holding facility for low-level criminals—mostly misdemeanor offenders or those awaiting trial for felonies. On paper, the place existed for short-term stays, but serious felony cases could stretch out months or even years. Inmates could get stuck here, spinning their wheels in legal purgatory, sharing space with all kinds of rivalries and unresolved street-level drama.

Jail vs. Prison: The Unyielding Filter

Compared to prisons—often built in rural areas where cheap local labor could handle the sprawling compounds—county jails were typically located right next to courthouses, making daily transports easier. But the real difference was that jails acted like a mandatory filter. Before you landed in prison, you passed through jail. Period. That was the system's design.

In-processing took anywhere from 12 to 24 hours, and my initiation started the moment I surrendered my street clothes. We were given apples and a steady stream of peanut butter and jelly sandwiches. Then came the gauntlet of screenings—medical, mental health, and gang affiliation—that determined how we'd be classified and which unit we'd call home.

The first screening was medical. They drew my blood and ran tests for sexually transmitted diseases, respiratory issues, diabetes—anything that could either spread through the jail's cramped quarters or require specialized treatment. Certain facilities couldn't handle chronic illnesses like Type I Diabetes. If you had that or something equally serious, they noted it carefully.

Child molesters presented a different type of risk. Everyone knew they were despised more than any other group. Between these walls, they became immediate prey—extorted for extra commissary, beaten, sexually abused, or subjected to all kinds of torment. Because arrest records were public, they couldn't hide their charges. It all went on file, and corrections staff had to decide if they needed protective custody to survive.

Mind Games: The Mental Health Assessment

Next up was a look into our heads. Jail served as a buffer to figure out if someone was truly mentally ill or just riding out a drug-fueled psychosis. From crack hallucinations to deeper psychiatric conditions, it mattered because certain inmates needed medical oversight or protective custody—especially those with developmental disabilities who'd be easy targets in this predatory environment.

As an addict myself, I knew that confusion all too well. I'd seen guys come in so intoxicated they were practically catatonic, only to snap back after a few days of forced sobriety. Sometimes that snap-back involved the realization of what they'd done to get locked up in the first place.

But the third screening—the gang affiliation check—was the real lynchpin for maintaining order. Chaos erupted fast if staff failed to keep known enemies apart. Nevada's prison and jail system, from my observation, primarily divided inmates along racial lines: Whites, Blacks, and Hispanics. Of these, the Whites tended to hold the most sway—likely because most of the guards were White too, though not all staff played favorites. Among White inmates, you'd see Aryan Brotherhood, Aryan Warriors, biker gangs like the Hells Angels, and other factions. Generations sometimes served time together —fathers and sons locked up simultaneously, perpetuating a warped legacy of criminal pride.

For Black inmates, it felt like there was no single unifying banner in the Nevada system. Folks from Oakland, Stockton, Sacramento, and all over California brought in Blood, Crip, Piru, Vice Lord, or Gangster Disciple affiliations. Lots of us ended up here on the full spectrum of charges—robbery, drug distribution, assault, you name it.

Hispanic inmates, meanwhile, largely split into two dominant groups: Norteños and Sureños. These two gangs hated each other enough to have standing orders to fight "on sight." Entire facilities leaned heavily toward one side for safety. At Northern Nevada Correctional Center, the Sureños ruled the yard. Hispanics also further separated themselves into "American-born" or "Paisa," referring to those directly from Mexico. Tattoos told each person's story—numbers, symbols, and block lettering marking sets or hometowns. A quick glance could mean the difference between who you approached and who you avoided.

Stripped of Dignity

After they cataloged my affiliations (or lack thereof), they stripped away my civilian life. I handed over everything—my clothes, shoes, wallet, and any dignity I had left. In exchange, I got a pair of flimsy flip-flops, undershirts, socks, and baggy jail scrubs. Then came the invasive part: naked, bend over, spread your cheeks, cough on command while someone in uniform watched. The idea was to prevent contraband, but mostly, it felt like a power move. Each facility had good guards and bad guards, but no matter who was on duty, that moment reduced you to your lowest form.

At Washoe County Jail, we had the "Killer B's"—three sheriff's deputies named Baltese, Beard, and Baker. All three had distinct personalities, and none were remotely friendly. Beard, the youngest, had a nasty habit of making inmates hold that bent-over position longer than necessary, as though feeding off the humiliation. Baker was the strictest—locking us down early, letting us out late, controlling our every movement with petty power plays. But Baltese was the most infamous among us. Built like a bodybuilder, he seemed to relish intimidation, hated by inmates and fellow officers alike.

In one especially ugly incident, Beard slammed me while I was in handcuffs, basically because I hadn't responded with the subservience he demanded. Nothing further came of it—no extra charges, no official discipline on my record. That was the worst part: the guards often faced no consequences for these power trips. The man was simply an asshole with a badge, and we all knew it.

Finding Routine in Chaos

Despite that, I tried to carve out some sense of normalcy. Each day in the jail had a rhythm: tier time, mealtime, then mandatory lockdowns. During lockdown, we'd be sealed in our cells while the guards roamed the corridor. When the cell doors finally buzzed open, some guys would just stay in their bunks, not wanting the headaches of dayroom politics. A few of us formed a loose group to exercise together—pull-ups, push-ups, dips, bodyweight squats—anything to keep our minds and bodies from rusting.

Parr Boulevard didn't have a massive yard. Instead, there was a cramped, triangular mini-yard enclosed by towering cement walls topped with chain-link fencing. At night, if you craned your neck just right, you might see a sliver of stars. That was our tiny window to the outside world. Inside, we had a communal dayroom with a single TV. The guards controlled its channels, so one moment we'd be stuck watching local news, and the next, they'd force us to watch nature documentaries about monarch butterflies. Some days it felt like mental torture. Other times, it was a blessed distraction.

Food in jail was generally bland but occasionally edible. Since the sheriff's wife secured the contract to provide meals, we joked that nepotism was alive and well. Still, if you had money in your commissary, you could buy real meals—burgers, shakes, fries—and these items became a form of currency. For broke guys like me, jail was extra dull. Money, or at least the promise of it, gave you leverage. Even behind bars, some people found ways to hustle—trading commissary items for "favors," whether extra phone time or a guard turning a blind eye.

The days in jail dragged. If you pleaded guilty, you might get shipped to prison in under 90 days, sometimes quicker. But if you fought your case, you could be there for two years or more. Federal cases could stretch four or five years, coiling tension and simmering grudges the entire time. And while any time spent in jail would count toward a prison sentence, that didn't make the waiting easier. Jail was unpredictable, stuffed with short-timers who brought street beefs inside. Contraband floated around—from drugs to shanks—hidden in every imaginable crevice. Guards occasionally performed "shakedowns," dumping our cells upside down to find anything we weren't supposed to have. They rarely found everything.

A Shattering Phone Call

One day, amidst my daily routine of waiting for legal news, my brother Michael reached out. His voice trembled as he told me my father—Sam—was dead. The man I'd viewed as a monster for so long, the root of my nightmares and resentments, was gone. He'd found sobriety in prison years before and apparently became a loving grandfather, or so my nephews experienced. I'd started to forgive him. I even tried building a new relationship from behind bars, but with me tangled in my own addiction, it never flourished.

When Michael spoke those words—"He's gone"—I felt everything and nothing all at once. Grief crushed me, and the tears flowed without shame. I cried like a child. Even after all the trauma and bitterness, I yearned for that reformed version of him. He'd become someone else's loving dad, and I'd missed it. For twenty-one years of my life, I'd drowned in crack and booze, trying to erase memories of those first eighteen years under his roof. Now I was stuck here, mourning the father I once believed incapable of goodness.

CHAPTER 10: MY REFLECTIONS

Jail can feel like an endless holding pattern—caught between the street and a looming prison sentence. Yet even in that cramped limbo, profound realizations emerge. When the news of my father's death reached me, I couldn't run or distract myself anymore. The steel bars forced me to confront a lifetime of hurt, regret, and complicated love. Jail isn't just a physical holding cell; it's also a mental one, where old wounds can finally surface.

1. **Environment Exposes Truth** - You can't hide behind illusions when you're locked up. The forced slowdown—limited TV, restricted movement—often lays your raw emotions bare, demanding real reflection.
2. **Guards and Power Plays** - Encounters with correctional officers reveal how easily authority can be misused. While some COs uphold integrity, others exploit their position. It's a stark reminder that who wields power matters.
3. **Gang Lines and Survival** - Racial affiliations and prison politics underscore how primal survival becomes behind bars. Picking a side or staying solo—both come with risks. Understanding these

social dynamics can mean the difference between safety and danger.

4. **Sorrow Mid-Sentence** - Losing a loved one—especially a complicated figure like Sam—creates emotional chaos. Incarceration strips away your usual coping methods, leaving no escape from the grief. Sometimes, that forced reckoning can spark deeper healing.
5. **Redefining Evil** - Within jail's walls, you'll meet people who've done horrific things. But are they inherently evil? Experience suggests many are broken, traumatized, and desperate. This doesn't excuse their crimes, but it widens your perspective on judgment and redemption.
6. **Facing Regrets** - The worst anguish isn't always the sentence—it's realizing the opportunities you wasted, the relationships left unresolved. Jail can become the place where you finally stop running and start owning those regrets.

CHAPTER 11
LOCKDOWN REALITIES-CONFLICTS & GROWTH

There is a prison sentencing hierarchy. At the very top is the death penalty, which is only given in extenuating circumstances, such as murder combined with rape, murder combined with robbery, or murder of a law enforcement officer. The death penalty sentence can sometimes be reduced to the next lower tier, which is Life Without the Possibility of Parole (LWO). LWO sentences always meant that no matter what age you were when you entered prison, you would only leave after dying there. These prisoners were often segregated from others because they were lifers with nothing to lose. They were not people to be trifled with—first, because whatever they did to get locked up in the first place was always seriously violent, and second, they couldn't possibly be sentenced to more time, which meant other lives simply weren't valued by them.

Lifers With the Possibility of Parole were next. After serving their minimum sentence, they'd come up for parole, and then every five years subsequent to that—at least in the Nevada system. They had hope.

Finally, most prison terms in Nevada are "indeterminate," meaning there is a range rather than a specified number of months or years.

The Reality of Sentencing

Indeterminate sentences are given in months, with an expectation that a person will serve at least their minimum number of months before an opportunity to appear before the parole board. For example, once I was sentenced to 16 to 72 months. That meant I would go before the parole board after 16 months at the earliest but could potentially serve six years (72 months) in prison if I had disciplinary problems. Usually, the most you would serve is about 55%, regardless of what we call your "top number," which is the maximum number of months (usually stated in years) that's reported in the media when they inform the public of someone's sentence.

Sentencing also varies based on whether the crime committed is a violation of state or federal law. Regarding parole, state sentences could be reduced by 40–50% for good behavior and other measures, whereas federal sentences were typically only reducible by 10%. For example, a person in Nevada sentenced to 60 to 120 months would be expected to serve five years before potentially being released on parole, or "on paper."

Appearing before a parole board to present your case for release is arguably the most important day for most inmates, as it literally determines if you'll be released, required to wait to appear again, or simply denied outright—something we called "getting dumped." My sentences were always indeterminate, meaning I'd appear at a parole hearing annually after serving my minimum months.

For someone who is not a convict or a repeat criminal offender, the only thing worse than a life sentence is a high bottom number. I've met men whose minimum sentence was over 40 years. Many men experience a profound moment of dread when the judge looks them in the eyes and tells them the minimum term they'll serve for the crime of which they've been convicted. Sentences such as 120 to 240 months were not unheard of, instantly signaling that life would be spent behind bars for at least the next 10 years—but could be extended through parole denials to 20 years minus any good time earned.

Prison Transfer

My transfer to prison was seamless the first time. It never occurred to me that this would be the first of three felony incarcerations that I, the Dartmouth College grad, would suffer over the next 10 years. I'd been charged, arraigned, pleaded guilty, and was subsequently sentenced to 12–34 months in prison for the internal possession of a controlled substance (remember what I called "walking while high"). I was more than ready to leave jail and have access to a larger space to stretch my legs. I found solace in knowing I could leave in as little as nine months with good time and would definitely be out in less than three years if I stayed out of trouble.

The bus ride over was subdued, with little talking. Some people were excited to enter prison for the first time, others were scared, and some were content to return "home." There were a few institutionalized prisoners, more comfortable navigating prison life than civilian life. I stepped off the bus, chained and wearing a tough face, though admittedly, I was scared. Soon, I was wearing prison-issue clothes and walking with a shaved head. I also had to shave my face—but with a dry, single-blade razor. Multiple-blade razors were prohibited for obvious reasons, but only God and the Warden knew why we couldn't have shaving cream or soap.

Any civilian attire or belongings I had were taken, kept safe until I was either released or died. Some prisoners were allowed to keep their civilian shoes but had to remove colored laces due to gang affiliations. I was sent to Northern Nevada Correctional Center (NNCC) for intake, then transferred to Warm Springs Correctional Center (WSCC) to finish my term. I was now housed with real killers, murderers, rapists, and other hardened criminals. Like the life I'd lived before this, I knew I just needed to learn and abide by the rules—the pre-existing scripts that maintained order. It's one thing to buck the system on the streets, where you can run or drive to another city or state to hide out. It's a completely different reality when there is nowhere—and I mean nowhere—you can hide for months or years on end, other than protective custody ("PC up"). Even the brightest candle's flame goes out when covered with a lid, and almost all new prisoners eventually capitulate and conform, just like every other prisoner who finds himself within those walls.

Life Inside

The very first lesson I learned was to show respect. Respect is the most important concept to understand—and many never learn it, paying a steep price. The first form of respect involved learning the prison power hierarchy and structure. At the very top of this pyramid, like a shining star atop a Christmas tree, was the individual inmate's prison sentence. It served as a control mechanism for those who wished to see the outside again or as a badge of power for those who never would—like the lifers without parole (LWOs) I mentioned earlier.

Just beneath that, barely perceptible, was the quality of an inmate's time, or rather, those who had the power to determine if each day was uneventful or landed you in the infirmary. This group included shot callers and those defined by their type of crime.

Still near the pinnacle was the Warden. It was their prison to run, their ship to captain, and he or she didn't mess around. The Warden had the essential voice of God, whether through explicit actions or implicitly turning a blind eye to enforcement proxies.

Beneath the Warden were the guards. They were the control arm, but more importantly, they acted as the Warden's buffer between chaos and order—the troops he commanded. They ruled by fear and intimidation, using tactics like frequent shakedowns, controlling yard time, determining jobs or roles, and, when necessary, wielding rifles or shotguns to subdue unruly inmates.

Usually beneath the guards were the Shot Callers, though in some prisons, they were the real power. These convicts, most often leaders in other capacities, ruled primarily through respect. They established rules of respect within their racial clique, and inmates either complied or sprinted to protective custody if they stepped out of line. Alliances between empowered guards and respected Shot Callers meant that for some, even protective custody wasn't safe enough.

One layer above the inmates themselves were the other prison administrators and civilian workers—people like counselors, clergymen, medical staff, and civilian workforce supervisors. Each played a role and, though usually lacking power to make your life hell, could help elevate you from it. A friendly counselor might elevate you to trustee status, offering a higher treatment level built on trust. A caring nurse might grant you an extended stay in the medical ward, allowing tensions in your unit to calm down, or help transfer you to a facility for aging inmates away from volatile younger prisoners.

The base of the entire pyramid, the foundation on which everything rested, was the inmates. Unified, we held temporary power. Divided, we had none. The idea portrayed in movies—that one guy could single-handedly take over a prison—was complete and utter nonsense. Never have I seen a "Billy Badass" who wasn't touchable or reachable. Granted, there were positions granted temporary asylum, but these always came at a cost and were always conditional. Anyone—absolutely anyone—who disturbed the mandated order on which a Warden's reputation rested could find themselves in a precarious position. As with any organization in history, the ultimate arbiter—the Grand Poobah through whom all decisions flowed—was always the entity controlling the purse strings, whoever that might be.

Rules Of The Game

At every level, there are rules. Upon my arrival at WSCC, one rule was instantly broken the first time I moved from intake unit to the yard at Warm Springs. The moment I stepped into my new cell my potential new bunkie looked up at me and said, "*you can't fucking bunk here.*" He was Aryan Brotherhood, tattoos and all, a sworn enemy of interracial mixing. In what world did the counselor assigning bunks put me in with a "*white*" thinking this was going to work? I went to the unit correctional officer (CO) but was told to deal with it. The counselor who'd assigned me to that cell was on leave and it would be at least four days before she returned so I just as quickly made the correct decision to go back to the intake unit and lockdown.

Prison is typically quiet. There are hundreds of men who have all manner of thoughts running through their minds. Some of them may be thinking something simple or nothing at all while others might be battling demons in their heads, the voices of those they've left in shallow graves or barrels of acid. With that understanding, one important rule is to Respect A Man's Quiet. My intake unit bunkie apparently didn't care about that rule as he listened to his radio without headphones. His radio annoyed the shit out of me. It was disrespectful but not worth stirring trouble over. He already had the bottom bunk which is generally the case for a senior person in a cell, so it wasn't a biggie for me to climb up. New to the scene, I kept my head down and mouth shut until I was moved to the correct cell on the yard when the counselor came back.

My new bunkie taught me the second rule. His name was Ronnie (died from drugs at age 26) a brother from Town Business (Oakland CA) who I got along great with. He was the one who taught me to Respect A Man's Space. Our cell was an approximately 80 square feet space that us two grown men would have to occupy together for the next 12-34 months while I served my sentence. The cell had a solid wall in the front with a steel door that had a hinged flap so food could be slid inside. The door slid horizontally and also had a window, approximately 4 x 24 inches. We were authorized a piece of cardboard to cover the window momentarily while we used the toilet which was stainless steel. Using it was about mutual respect. We'd notify the other that we needed the bathroom and the other would turn away and mind his business. I liked Ronnie's rule that we'd wipe down the toilet after each use. It meant I never had to sit on another man's piss. There was a small stainless steel mirror affixed to the wall, but it was barely usable as it was scratched up. There was also a small closet that was shared 50/50. In it were our bins, clothing, food items, cleaning supplies and toiletries. If a person could afford it, they could buy a small television to keep inside the cell, though they were supposed to wear headphones when watching it. I've never portrayed myself as a thug or badass. I would fight as a last resort but have never fancied or labeled myself as a fighter and felt no need to puff up at Ronnie or prove something. I had no qualms about respecting Ronnie's space, and he always respected mine. His rules were fine because, in spite of the examples I'd set by destroying my life, I'm an incredibly organized man. I prefer things in their place, *mise en place* as the French would say. Cleanliness was akin to a love language for me so I knew Ronnie and I would get along well. I took pride in having one of the neatest, cleanest and most ordered living areas on the whole yard. Order for me means control and at least I could control this small adjacent area of my cell or later on dorm areas.

As he showed me around the cell, the third rule came quickly. It was simply Never Touch A Man's Possessions Without Permission. Our closet space was shared but each man had his own 2' x 3' yellow bin. They were lockable but Ronnie wanted a bunkie that wouldn't force him to need a lock. Leaving it unlocked with the doors open was a different story but, between us, trust via respect was paramount. Fourth, Never Sit On Another Man's Bunk Without Permission. It was disrespectful to have your ass where another man lays his head. One day, as we played cards while chilling in the cell during Closed Time, I learned the fifth rule after I violated it. Having just won a laid 20 points while playing dominos, I slammed my domino down and shouted to

Ronnie, "*That's twenty on your bitch ass!*" Anyone that has been in prison before can tell you something I came to learn in seconds after my mistake, Never Call A Man Out Of His Name, especially not words that cause an insta-ass whooping like bitch, punk, faggot, racial slurs, or pussy. As Ronnie quickly stood up and closed the cardboard flap on the door, I started pleading. Really and truly, I didn't mean any disrespect but that didn't matter. The script is very clear on this rule. If Ronnie let me get away with calling him a bitch then I'd view him like a bitch and treat him like a bitch which would then lead to him being my bitch. He had to immediately rectify the situation and I was about to have a really bad night. Hands in the air, speaking as fast and calmly as I could, I apologized like a motherfucker. It wasn't about me showing weakness. Just the opposite. I'd messed up. I'd truly overstepped a core tenant and his reaction told me I'd messed up. My only saving grace, the only thing that kept me from what surely was going to be an ass whooping, is it was just us two in the cell and no one else heard it. I had also known Ronnie on the streets of Reno and we were cool there also in my favor. If I had exhibited my naiveté in front of others, I would have surely been monkey-stomped.

Rule six, if it hasn't been guessed, is Man Up. When a mistake has been made or an action taken by you, it was better if you owned up to it and/or be prepared to knuckle-up if that was a consequence. If you didn't stand on your word then you couldn't be trusted and people that can't be trusted aren't in the circle. However, scuffles were to be avoided if possible as a provision under the next rule which was Send It

Up The Flag Pole to the Shot Callers. A couple of knuckleheads fighting over a stepped on shoe or misplaced word could cause a total lockdown and everyone would have to return to their cells for an indeterminate amount of time, missing commissary, sports, sunshine and especially visitation. If you want to forget how to walk, shower, or eat comfortably or experience never feeling safe for months on end, start a fight/riot or do something else stupid in prison that causes everyone to suffer. Whoever said hell hath no fury like a woman scorned has never seen 500 inmates pissed off at and plotting ways to get back at one or two idiots that cost them their visitation with family, their access to the yard, or their ability to watch a TV for a three week. Problems were to be sent up to the Shot Callers and they'd handle it in ways that didn't involve everyone getting locked down.

Other rules included things like Never Asking A Man What He's In For. If he wanted you to know, he'd tell you. If you wanted to really know ask someone on the outside to look it up in the system, its public knowledge. Don't dabble in drugs, sex, or gambling unless you can handle the consequences. Unlike the street where there are a plethora of ways to support your addiction, in the confines of prison there are very few options and the deeper the debt, the more expensive the cost would become to a person's dignity. Unlike jail, the primary trading currency in the Nevada prison system was postage stamps. Owing someone too many stamps could result in everything from sanctioned violence to indentured servitude or forcefully involuntary sexual acts. Though I've never witnessed a rape while I was in, there were definitely sexual acts accepted in lieu of payment. Though people keep quiet, prison has few secrets and once you've crossed a line you've set a new precedent.

The Hustle Of Prison

Stamps were typically earned by hustling. There were various things people did to earn prison currency or stamps, and everyone knew you Never Mess Up Another Man's Hustle. Prison has an entire underground economy. An example would be people that worked in the kitchen sneaking out supplies for sale to others. Things like sugar were very high value as it was a vital ingredient in hooch. Coffee, snacks, and cigarettes were also staples because people loved everything from coffee so thick we called it mud to honey buns and sweet. Some guys operated little stores with items that couldn't be acquired from the commissary. Things like little snack cakes we called zoom zooms and wham whams were a hot commodity along with coffee cakes. Some inmates performed the prison equivalent of laundry cleaning services as there were many inmates who didn't know how, did not want to or had never done their own laundry. Laundry was done in bulk by the prison but many people had items come up missing, so they preferred a more individualized service. There were men who would rather go to the hole than make their beds, so some guys cleaned cells for others as a hustle while others had more serious hustles like selling drugs or manufacturing hooch. A few of the lifers were able to have little gardens and they sold their produce. There were no shortage of effeminate gay men in there, interestingly though more Blacks. They could also be found braiding hair, sewing or mending clothes, and performing various consensual sex acts. Men would just dip into a cell and put the cardboard over the window.

Likely the biggest hustle was gambling. With limited options in a confined space, people found ways to bet on just about anything in the sporting world. Many millions of stamps have changed hands over NFL games. I was educated and got along with most everyone. I could hold conversations with any staff member, let alone the inmates so my hustles usually revolved around educational tasks like tutoring and writing letters for other Black inmates. Beyond the hustle, we were all assigned jobs in prison, categorized by "*pay number*". The pay number was essentially a chart that detailed the pay scale for various job titles. The best job for non-lifers was working in the snack bar. The inmate workers there were limited to 5 inmates, two white, two Hispanic, and one Black. That was the balance, and it was overseen by a civilian worker. I was approached one day by the Black shot caller and was offered the position, he appreciated my intelligence and that I would write letters for Black men that could not read or write (until prison I had never knowingly met a man who was illiterate, but I was to meet many while incarcerated over the years).

Adjusting To The New

Following the rules came easy for me. I knew I didn't have long to serve, and I didn't want to stay a day later than I had to. I stayed clean and was very excited to be on a yard that had a basketball court and other sports. I began to get serious about lifting weights and my fitness. It was mostly Blacks and Whites that lifted weights as Hispanics preferred calisthenics and bodyweight resistance style exercises. They exercised in groups reminiscent of military units doing physical training in the morning with someone calling cadence to maintain uniformity.

I fell in love with weight lifting and especially power lifting. I lifted every day I could, without fail, until the competition where I was able to do a deadlift of 505 lbs while weighing 198lbs. More weight was added, and on my next lift my left shoulder popped out of socket. Feeling the pain when I completed the lift, I was a mess but I loved it and earned a lot of respect from my fellow inmates because I finished the lift . I was viewed as a solid dude and since I avoided all the political and financial traps, people knew I had a level head. I was approached by a Black shot caller who offered me a job in the snack bar. I gladly accepted and thus leveled up as my peers really valued my work ethic and skills in sports.

When I wasn't lifting, working, or hustling, I could usually be found on the basketball court hooping or on the fields playing softball. I was the MVP when my team won the over 40 basketball championship and I came in second place in the softball league home run hitting contest. I was known as a homerun hitter, literally and figuratively which afforded me an easy stint. My paperwork was solid and any inquiring eyes could read for themselves the circumstances under which I'd come to prison. I never got into a fight, never had anything stolen from me, and was never called out of my name. Not once. Respect is paramount in prison. It's earned daily in microtransactions as nothing goes unnoticed when you have hundreds of sets of eyes observing everything. I built my reputation just as every other person did, moment by defining moment measured over time.

I entered the Nevada prison system as an alcoholic drug addict who repeatedly committed stupid low-level crimes to support my habit. While incarcerated, I lost my fear of prison because I learned how to navigate the various rules at play. I knew how to earn and maintain respect non-violently and I knew how to take care of myself. I remained clean and thus level headed. I appeared before my parole board. They wanted to know my release plan, a plan developed by the inmate and his counselors to protect society from their misgivings more than to set the inmate up for success. I expounded on how I'd remained clean and would use my God given intellect to keep my life on track since I'd already gotten myself there with the helpful intervention of the State. Even as I sat there, I questioned myself internally. Yes, I possessed the gift of talk, but I'd developed a general anxiety around my release, wondering if this time would be different. I was nervously asking myself and trying to answer honestly if I wanted it to be different.

The parole board was happy with my verbalized

responses and was granted a release back to the world with a date 2-3 months away. Since I was being released early, I'd be released on parole versus having served my full sentence or "*expiring my sentence*". Knowing I was being released was an amazing feeling. I'd been approved for parole on my first try and, although I had to live within certain guidelines like reporting weekly, not using drugs, and not living with another person on parole, I was content in knowledge that this time it would be different. It always comes back to that famous cliché "*everyone has a plan in the ring (world) until they get hit the first time!*" Yes I had a plan...

Wide Awake

Sitting in my cell over the next 3 months, my focus became clear. My thought pattern evolved, and I took account of what I had going for me. I was sober. I was Ivy league educated. I had years of knowledge of how the streets worked and, having tutored several brothers on the inside, I saw an opportunity to better my position in life. Night after night my dream would visit me until it also occupied my daydreams. What had begun as a silent musing had morphed and was now fully developed. I had an idea, perhaps my best ever!

My father had left me a small inheritance when he passed. Michael had been managing the funds for me and I knew I had $20,000 to use as start-up capital for my new venture. It was quite a gift and I was excited, knowing I was blessed with another opportunity to start over. It was going to be great. I would use my $20,000 to secure inventory, a location, minimal staffing, and become a wholesale distributor of drugs. I wanted to use my Dartmouth intelligence and my street smart to become a drug kingpin in Reno, NV. I'd been risking my life over literal coins, playing it small with reckless abandon. If I executed my plan properly, 2002 would be my year, Ken Miller's year, to step into the big leagues in the drug world!

The time came for my release. In all my thoughts over that three month waiting period, there wasn't a day where I believed I'd remain sober. I knew I was going to have some cold beer and I knew I was going to chase a ringer. I also figured I'd be able to manage it this time because I'd learned so much, gleaned so many tips from these incarcerated professionals I'd just served time with. I was smarter than them and smarter than I had been previously on the streets. I entered the Nevada system as an alcoholic drug addict who committed crimes, an inmate if you will. I was certified now. I'd leveled up and would now commit crimes as a way of life, my method of ascension to greatness. I was leaving the Nevada system as a convict.

I finished my exit exams and conducted the exit inventory. Prisoners were not allowed to take state owned property with them so all I had were the clothes I wore into jail when I turned myself in. They wouldn't even allow me to keep my prison issue boxers or socks. They handed me a small box with everything I owned, issued me a check for $23 and a bus ticket, gave me instructions on when and where to report for parole compliance, and dropped me off at a bus station in downtown Carson City, NV. Unlike jail which releases you at

1-2am during prime street hustle time, it was the middle of the day when I stepped out of the prison van and I was a free man. That night, for the first time since my arrest, I saw the night sky. It's amazing the things you don't realize you'd miss or have missed until reminded.

No Time For Second Chances

Leaving the bus station back in Reno, I knew two things: I was hungry, and I wasn't going to report to my parole officer. My first order of business was to stop in my favorite casino, the Cal Neva, and order my favorite breakfast: two eggs, toast, hash browns, bacon, and an ice-cold beer. I cashed the pittance the state had given me and received some additional drink tokens while I sat alone, plotting and planning. I remembered just how low I'd gotten after robbing my mom and swallowing those pills to end the pain. Here, as I sat now, I'd been granted life after death and vowed to make the best of it. It was time for me to make a name for myself.

At the time, my name on the streets of Reno was Alaska, but it wasn't well known. To make a kingpin-level name for myself, I figured I'd use the ten-step guide left by fellow New Yorker Christopher Wallace, who went by the street name The Notorious BIG. His list, released via his song "The Ten Crack Commandments," included:

1. Never let anyone know how much money you have.
2. Never let anyone know your next move.

3. Never trust anyone.
4. Never use the product you sell.
5. Never sell where you live.
6. Never take credit.
7. Keep your family and business completely separated.
8. Never keep any crack on you.
9. If you aren't being arrested, stay away from police.
10. Consignment is not for novices

Leaving the casino that day, my first step was to call Michael and have him wire me $5,000. At the time, Reno was undergoing a real estate boom as many Californians were taking out home equity lines of credit to buy much cheaper housing in Nevada for use as rental properties or vacation homes. Some larger developers had banded together and were renovating two or three old hotels in the area. I took the $5,000 Michael had wired me and bought two weeks' stay in one of those hotels, as they were being offered at a substantial discount due to construction. Additionally, I had an entire floor to myself, as no tourists wanted to deal with the mess.

I met a girl, Darlene, and we started partying. She was an alcoholic Native American working girl (she died from her alcoholism within two years of our meeting), and we got along great. I told her my big dreams and the vision I'd execute to bring it all to life. She was down for the cause, and our journey together began. I bought a second room and hired two girls to turn tricks there. They were next door to me, so I could monitor operations from my room. Having already secured a place to stay, a partner, and a small workforce, I bought an ounce of crack cocaine, and my plan was working.

Darlene began smoking the crack and wanted some ice from the machine to make a cold drink. I threw her a t-shirt, and she walked her scantily clothed self out of the room. Coming back, she said she didn't know where the machine was, so I quickly donned a pair of boxers and a t-shirt to show her. We got the ice, but when we returned to our room, we both realized we had a problem. Standing there in my boxers, with her looking at me in my t-shirt, we asked each other if we'd grabbed a key. Neither had, and we were locked out.

We managed to call security from a phone in the hall. When security arrived, they asked a few questions. My embarrassment turned to fear when they unlocked the door. Peeping in quickly, I saw cash and baggies of crack spread all over the room. Security needed to enter the room to check my ID and ensure everything was okay, so I quickly brushed past them, talking my ass off and hiding all I could. It was a close call, but we made it. Day one of my kingpin ascension was a success. To celebrate, we smoked some more.

Two days later, I'd completely blown through $5,000. The four of us had smoked an entire ounce of crack before purchasing and smoking everything else we could. I wasn't worried, though, and called Michael to wire me another $5,000, which he did. Darlene managed to sell a rock, and we had our first success. While many other businesses frame their first dollar on the wall, we simply had a party.

No one smokes that much crack without getting noticed

in downtown Reno. I'm not sure which one of my girls opened their mouth, but soon word was spreading about how much cash I had. Suddenly, I was very popular and had a lot of friends. My crew, my new friends, and I partied and smoked another $5,000 in crack before my rental period was over. I had an idea—I needed a larger amount of crack, so I went and purchased some on consignment from a plug. With my rising popularity, I knew I'd be able to move all the product, as I'd just watched nearly $10,000 worth get smoked in a week and a half.

Darlene and I continued plotting together and had now been lovers for almost two weeks, so things were obviously serious between us. We lost control a little and smoked the entire batch I'd secured on consignment. That was a turning point, as my paranoia was now validated by the reality that I owed a substantial amount of money to this drug dealer, a real wholesaler, and I needed to pay up immediately. I called Michael, only this time I let him know unequivocally: "Michael, don't send me any money after this. If you send me any more money, another dollar, you'll kill me. Mike, I will die. I'll either overdose or someone will kill me for the cash!" He understood. He wired me the last money, I paid my debt, and was flat broke again.

Having survived a near-death experience, Darlene and I were smoking a lot and both paranoid. I'd secured another room, away from the chaos I'd created by having all that money and dope. While walking across the room to turn on the light, I hit my knee on the corner of the bed. I felt warmth and wetness running down my leg. When I turned on the light, I saw an inch-long gash on my knee. I was bleeding like a stuck pig and began frantically searching for a bandage or something to stop the blood. I had blood all over the room, between the bed and the light switch. I didn't know a knee could bleed so profusely.

With no bandage in sight and the blood refusing to stop, I grabbed one of my dirty socks from the ground and wrapped my knee with it, tying it like a pressure bandage. The bleeding stopped, and I was relieved, but it still throbbed painfully. I lay down to take the pressure off of it and woke up four or five hours later in intense pain. Looking down, I saw my knee had swollen substantially, and I was unable to bend it. Any attempt I made to apply pressure was met with instant, debilitating pain. Confused about what was happening, I called Mom. She arrived shortly after, and I elevated my leg in the backseat, writhing in pain, as she drove me to the emergency room. Apparently, in the short time I'd worn the sock I'd used to wrap the wound, my knee had become severely infected. At the ER, I was given antibiotics and mild pain medication. I hated that my mom had to see me this way again, but I needed her help.

My entire plan of becoming a drug kingpin had unraveled and fallen apart. My dreams and aspirations went up in smoke—literally— aided by Brillo pads and Bic lighters. Out of the ten simple rules Biggie Smalls cautioned me to follow, I'd violated eight within my first week in business, and it cost me the entire operation. Broke and broken, I was once again homeless and spiraling out of control. My partner in crime, Darlene, lost faith in me as I lay bedridden while my knee healed. After letting me know how poor of a provider I was, she broke up with me and hit the stroll again. We were together less than one month.

Life Of A Hustler

My mom made sure I had something to eat, and once I was able to walk again, I went back to the streets. I was tweaking, and once that started, it was on and popping. I was in and out of missions, sleeping in abandoned cars, empty rental properties with other squatters, and anywhere else I could uncomfortably lay my head. I returned to what I knew best: crack-driven hustling. I began with panhandling, as my greatest skill was sales.

Sales has always come naturally to me. Selling is simply soliciting an entity to provide money or goods. The two primary components are content (what you say) and delivery (how you say it). What you say matters. When panhandling or otherwise asking for money, if you ask for "change," that's exactly what you'll get. There's an old adage about a closed mouth not getting fed, but they forgot to add, "Always ask for what you want." It's true that you might just get what you've asked for, and it's your own fault if you end up disappointed. I always chose honesty and transparency. Instead of trying to feign needing a bus pass or food for my kids, as many women did, I'd say directly that I wanted money to buy alcohol. Sometimes people would even return and bring a drink or food if that's what I needed, especially if they also drank. I always did my best to balance my appearance between presentable and disheveled. If I were too clean, people thought I was a scammer and wouldn't give me anything. If I were too filthy, they wouldn't roll down their windows or approach me on the street for fear of catching some disease. It was also imperative to maintain a non-threatening posture, with welcoming and disarming eyes where possible.

I was always cognizant of being a tall Black male when approaching any person or vehicle. The demographic makeup of a vehicle's occupants mattered, and I'd gotten it down to a science. I never approached Asians because, in my experience, they typically didn't give anything. They'd usually pretend not to speak English and walk off. I stopped asking older Black women as well. Many of them seemed either angry or saddened to see me begging, especially if they'd just come off a long night shift or something. They'd often give advice like, "Baby, you don't need to be on these streets." Older White women usually appeared fearful or threatened. Sometimes I could hear an audible gasp and watch them recoil as I approached, staring straight ahead as if I were invisible.

Although young white females were a decent demographic to approach, the absolute best group for me was always young white males in their 20s and 30s. Usually in town to party and carrying extra cash, they typically weren't afraid. College students, especially frat types, were great targets. I preferred single people or pairs, as larger groups tended to be too focused on partying, whereas an individual or couple might discreetly slide me a few dollars. I could also solicit them further to ask if there was anything else they needed. Young white men often wanted to impress their female companions, meaning they either bluntly told me to go away or were very charitable, depending on the girl's attitude. People who'd been drinking tended to be more giving than sober folks. Occasionally, a slightly intoxicated person would hand me a $20 bill, making for a great night since my goal was always at least $1 for my $0.93 Natural Ice beer and $10 for a piece of crack.

Timing was crucial. The highest traffic times were around 4–5 p.m., as people headed home after work, and again at about 2 a.m., when many men were gambling, drunk, and seeking sex or drugs. The streets operated on their own clock, and there were specific times ideal for hustling. There's no hustle at 9 a.m.; the streets are quiet, almost serene. Parks seem harmless, and corner lots look like legitimate parking businesses. A certain hum is missing from the sidewalks—no shuffling, no low voices, no long silk legs coming toward you, no bodies leaning against walls. But come 4 p.m., as the day wound down, the hustle started up again, and the night came alive. By 6 p.m., it was game time. Thursday, Friday, and Saturday brought in out-of-towners. This was the pre-cell phone and pre-swipe era.

When panhandling wasn't cutting it, I resorted to petty crimes. I'd work the casinos, stealing buckets of change people left unattended at slot machines or swiping tips off restaurant tables. I always felt guilty about that because I knew the servers worked their asses off. If a cashier turned away, I'd slip money from the till or perform general shenanigans to take advantage of obviously intoxicated people. Occasionally, I'd shoplift liquor, cigarettes, or food items. I'd often walk the gaming floors looking down, as people frequently dropped money or left winnings in machines. As last resorts, if hungry enough, I'd dine and dash or occasionally commit muggings, though very infrequently.

Bottom line: I was an addict with an addiction to support. Once alcohol entered my system, my "fuck-its" activated, and I'd start tweaking for cocaine, doing anything necessary to find it, including searching sidewalks frequented by addicts for anything resembling crack rocks. Several times, I picked up crack-like items on Reno's sidewalks, took them back to the motel, and lit them to see if they melted. On at least two occasions, I successfully found crack this way.

My street hustles were mostly confined to what we called the "little loop," a two-block-by-four-block area in Reno, and the "big loop," a four-block-by-eight-block area. Everything was based around the nearby motels. Each day, I'd walk my loops looking for opportunities to make money or acquire drugs—ideally both. My daily goal was always payment in money or drugs. As a crack addict, I needed money for rock. As a hustler, it was my job to supply something desired. I acquired knowledge or goods people valued. In another life, I might have been a high-end outside salesman or a procurement specialist. Whatever my clients needed—whether locals or tourists—my job was to secure it: drugs, alcohol, girls, guys, or a location (better known as a "spot"). Whatever reason they had, they relied on me to heighten their experience. And I gladly did so, for a price.

I routinely posted up at a regular location, and people

would find me. Those who knew me would start off the interaction with, "I got twenty," or, "I got fitty." They knew I understood their language. Locals and regulars knew who was posted where, and since I'd learned early not to rip people off, I quickly developed a consistent stream of regulars. As dusk encroached, the call-and-response would ensue. My loops would begin, and as two bodies passed, the familiar cadence —"What's up?" "What's up?"—initiated our usual exchange. Passing by on my loop, I'd acknowledge the people I saw with a quick, "You alright?" "You looking?" or simply, "What's up?" It was the evening's preliminary relay. Faster than their verbal answers, their eyes usually gave the response. Those tweaking were easy to spot immediately. Local guys, out of their normal areas trying to be discreet, and regulars waiting for me to offer my services, all appeared more frequently the lower the sun sank in the sky. It was a game of reading people, watching their eyes, and observing their discretion. My responses came in short forms: "Black or white (woman)?" "Girl or guy?" "Crack, heroin, or weed?" "Drinks or spots?" "Where you at?" "Where you staying?" "Gimme a half hour—I'll come to you." I've repeated these lines more times than I can count.

I was also a skilled and trusted drug runner. Not only did I work on behalf of clients, but I also ran for the dealers. I tried to stick with dealers I already knew or who had verified me, but that wasn't always possible. The drug dealers lived by the same scripts, though, and were justifiably cautious of being robbed or infiltrated by law enforcement. When I'd enter a place on behalf of a client, they'd challenge me, suspecting I might be a cop. My go-to response, which doubled as an additional hustle, was, "Shit, give me a rock and I'll smoke that motherfucker right now." Cops weren't allowed to smoke crack, and I always kept a pipe ready in my sock. They'd give me a hit, and I'd smoke my crack as they continued smoking their ever-present weed. Sometimes they'd request an additional step, and I'd have to show them my junk since cops weren't likely to comply with such a demeaning request. Usually, if I was bringing a new client, the D-boy would break me off with an extra rock as a token of appreciation, which I welcomed. Their wholesale price was only about $3 per rock, so it was easy for them to pass along a little extra motivation to me—no different than buying a great restaurant server a spiced chai latte before a shift. For the client, I'd usually say I could get three good rocks for $50, when in reality, I would get four and pocket one. There were times I could smoke one rock for validation, receive one rock as appreciation, acquire one rock as a tax, and then get a tip from the client for delivering three quality rocks. Hustlers hustle, just like cheaters cheat and singers sing. The same respect I had in the penitentiary extended to the streets for those who knew me. Sure, I'd done some scandalous things and occasionally ripped off an unsuspecting drug dealer or naive client, but they hadn't caught me, so my name was intact. Better, it was solid.

Pit Of Despair

I was always searching for angles to hustle, and no one was immune. Hell, I even realized a common problem many crack addicts had: once we started smoking, just like I'd done countless times, we'd get stuck in whatever little place we were smoking. Most often, we smoked in common motel rooms, making it easy for me to knock on a door and ask if anyone needed anything. They'd request new setups from the corner store or any element of them. I'd run over and grab the little glass straight shooters next to the registers that had fake roses in them. Everyone knew those were sold to crack smokers, but capitalism dictated turning a blind eye. Sometimes they needed Brillo pads, lighters, beer, liquor, girls, or whatever else. For me, it didn't matter. I had a habit to support.

As one of the few men working the streets as a prostitute —especially a good-looking one—if clients wanted male companionship, I'd step up and take the trick. If I could, I always angled to turn the trick into a mark, no differently than the girls would. Whatever combination of drugs they wanted, I'd run and get it, then come back and take care of whatever else they needed. About 80% of the men I encountered were looking for women. Though white women were easier to find, black girls could also be located if clients used my services because I knew exactly where to look for them. About 10% of the men specifically wanted another man, and the remaining 10% didn't care either way—they just wanted to get wasted and have a good time. Who cared if the sex was from a man or a woman?

I kept hustling and stayed high. One night while I was out, a vehicle pulled up beside me. A white couple sat inside, and the woman asked, "Hey, if we paid you, would you fuck me while he watches?" I said sure and got in with them. We wanted to get some drinks first, so they pulled into a convenience store, handed me cash, and I ran inside to grab beer. There was quite a long and slow-moving line. Impatient, I decided to just take the case of beer and walk out. I knew that store well, and they didn't have an alarm. As I walked out, almost back to the car, I was grabbed by a man who turned out to be an off-duty cop moonlighting as store security. I was arrested, but I was more upset that I didn't get to party with the couple, who I'm sure had no trouble finding another willing participant.

A Temporary Lifeline

While in-processing at Parr Blvd., I was told I had an outstanding warrant for my arrest. My decision to not report to my parole officer (PO) was obviously a violation of Nevada law, and I had to appear before a Parole Violation Hearing. Apparently, a warrant had been issued shortly after Darlene and I had split. During about 90% of my time free, the police were trying to track me down, but I'd managed to avoid getting caught for petty crimes. At the hearing, I gave as many decent-sounding excuses as I could but ultimately decided the best thing was to man up and stand accountable. "You know what, I have no excuse, Your Honor. I should have reported." I submitted a urinalysis, and my case was transferred back to Drug Court.

In Drug Court, I was remanded to the Center Street Mission again to undergo their treatment program. They gave me an ankle monitor to track my movements and placed me under house arrest. At the Mission, I was warned clearly: "Mr.

Miller, there is a mandatory curfew from 6 p.m. to 6 a.m., during which you are confined to these grounds. Any violation of this is considered an escape from custody. You're allowed to work, but there is zero tolerance for substance use —drugs or alcohol. Upon re-entry, you'll be breathalyzed and subjected to random urine testing. Any violation of these rules will be considered a violation of the Court's order, and you'll go back to prison. Do you understand?" I shrugged yes and began treatment again.

Left Broken & Beaten

I began working at Labor Ready, doing temporary day labor jobs. I needed to be paid above the table to show proof of employment. After nearly two weeks of hard work, I received my paycheck on a Friday. That night, a cold beer and crack called my name, though I didn't take a full dive. I returned to the Mission the next morning and contacted my PO. It had been 12 hours. My PO sounded disappointed but understanding. He respected that I'd manned up and initiated contact on my own. He told me, "No problem, just come on down, and we'll clean up some paperwork, then send you back on house arrest." Arriving shortly after, I was arrested for violating parole and returned to jail.

Not only had I failed to report to my PO, but I'd also tested positive for cocaine in my urine and violated curfew at the Mission. I was sentenced to serve the remainder of my time for violating parole and was sent once again to NNCC in Carson City. This time, I wasn't transferred anywhere else because I'd also picked up the charge for escaping from house arrest, which made me a flight risk. In Nevada, when you escape the parameters of your house arrest, it isn't considered just a minor violation—it's treated as if you'd scaled the walls at Nevada State Penitentiary or another high-security facility. Any time that I would serve from that day forward would be in medium-security prisons.

While doing intake into the prison, I again entered what's called the Fish Tank—the area and process where prisoners are held during the assessment period to determine how to categorize them. Whereas I'd been celled with Ronnie the first time, now I had a cool older brother who turned out to be the sibling of a famous drug kingpin in DC named Rayful Edmond. He shared his story of having been a low-level wholesale drug runner for his brother, who was the largest dealer in DC during the late 1980s. He was a crack addict himself, and one day, while partying with a street-working girl he had met, he apparently hadn't heeded Biggie Smalls' advice either. He was so high on his own supply that he didn't observe the girl setting him up to get robbed. She left to purchase cigarettes (Kool menthols, I'm sure!), and the robbers returned with her. They subdued him, tied him up, took his drugs and money, and then drove him away with the intent to kill and dump the body.

While subdued, he'd repeatedly mentioned who his brother was, but in the heat of the moment, the robbers paid no attention. Driving down the highway toward death, one of the robbers turned to him and asked, "Did you say you're Rayful Edmond's brother?" He said yes. The car soon stopped on the side of the road, and they dumped him out, speeding away after explaining that the girl never told them who he was—just that he had drugs and money. Listening to him, I was thankful I hadn't been robbed during my very short-lived kingpin shenanigans. He became a key witness after flipping for the feds. They placed him in witness protection and shipped him off to Kansas with a new name, complete identity, and stipend to help him start fresh—but he was an addict. Like the many opportunities at a new life I'd squandered, he relapsed into addiction, and they eventually kicked him out of the program since he was now a liability given the secrets he possessed.

His brother, Rayful Edmond III, was a notorious drug kingpin who ran the largest drug distribution operation in Washington, DC, during the height of the War on Drugs. Rayful was the real deal. For context, US Attorney Eric Holder —who later became Attorney General of the United States under President Obama—remarked that Rayful Edmond had become an even more prolific drug dealer in prison than he ever had been on the streets, despite already having been the largest distributor of cocaine in DC history. Sharing a cell with his brother, I realized just how much of a drug kingpin I was not. I did my time without incident and was released.

Returning to the streets from prison once again broke me. I was physically, spiritually, mentally, and emotionally depleted. I fell so deep and spiraled so hard this time that I couldn't make it to a mission or shelter most nights. I became the poster child for what crack cocaine addiction could do to a person's life. As I used more and more, chasing a ringer, my body rapidly deteriorated with visible weight loss, pronounced paranoia, and incessant skin rashes. If I wasn't living in a large cement pipe I'd discovered, I found shelter in abandoned vehicles. One day, I stumbled upon two unoccupied homes and began squatting in them, using them as my base of operations for prostitution. I had turned myself into a pure survivalist, relying 100% on street life to sustain myself.

CHAPTER 11: MY REFLECTIONS

Walking into prison for the first time is a shock, but walking out can be just as disorienting. The world doesn't pause while you're locked up. It moves on, leaving you to figure out where you fit once you're back on the outside. But the real battle isn't against the system—it's against yourself. The old patterns don't disappear just because you've done time. The same temptations, the same cycles, the same fast money and easy escapes are all waiting, just as you left them. The difference comes down to whether you fall back into the script or finally decide to flip the page.

1. **The Prison You Carry** - Prison doesn't start with shackles or end with a release date. It's a mindset, a conditioning of survival that lingers long after you walk free. The rules of the yard shape you, the hierarchy embeds itself in your instincts, and respect becomes currency. If you don't unlearn that conditioning, the outside world feels like another trap, just with looser bars.
2. **Respect Isn't Just A Word** - In prison, respect is law. It's not just about pride—it's about survival. A single misstep, an unintended slight, can set off a chain reaction that costs you your safety, your

dignity, or worse. But respect isn't only about fear. It's about order. It's about the delicate balance that keeps hundreds of volatile men from tearing each other apart. And in the free world, that balance still exists—it's just dressed up in suits, handshakes, and silent understandings.

3. **The Currency of Consequences** - The system doesn't care about your intentions, your regrets, or your realizations. Once you step into that courtroom, you're a case number, a record, a repeat offender. And when your rap sheet reads like a resume of recklessness, mercy runs dry. The choices you make—inside and outside—accumulate interest. Some debts you pay with time, others with blood, and the rest with whatever scraps of self-respect you have left.
4. **The Hustle Never Ends—But It Can Change** - There's always a game to play. Whether it's the underground economy of prison or the street hustle of Reno, the core principles stay the same: supply, demand, and who controls what. The real question is whether you stay a pawn or learn to play a different board. The same intelligence that fuels survival in the yard can build something better outside—but only if you stop using it to con yourself first.
5. **No One Escapes Alone** - Every man in prison learns this: solitary strength is a myth. Even the toughest lifers rely on networks, on alliances, on

the unspoken bonds that make survival possible. The free world isn't any different. The difference is, out here, those bonds don't have to be built on fear. Finding real allies—mentors, friends, people who see past the mistakes—can be the only thing standing between another relapse and a real future.

6. **Freedom Requires a New Script** - You don't walk out of prison free. You walk out with a choice: keep following the same script that led you back inside, or rewrite the damn thing. And rewriting it? That's the real test. Because once you know the rules of one world, it's easy to fall back into them. It's easy to believe you were made for it. But real freedom means tearing up that script, even when every muscle memory, every instinct, every old temptation tells you to follow the lines you've always known.

CHAPTER 12
SPIRITUAL SURRENDER & SELF-INVETOR

In the fall of 2004, I met a "trick" I planned on converting into a regular "mark." I was in such a bad way, both physically and emotionally, that earning a few dollars off a new man seemed like a small light in a dark tunnel. What I didn't realize was that he saw right through my façade. He recognized the grim, ghost-like figure I'd become, though we'd never met, and he felt compelled to help restore some part of me that was still human.

A Brief Respite Named Eugene

Truthfully, I was at rock bottom. My addiction had rendered me so unkempt and foul-smelling that even paying clients wanted nothing to do with me. Nobody desired to be near me in that condition. But this particular man—whose name was Eugene—stepped in like a silent lifeguard. He offered me a shower, a meal, and the chance to feel the warmth of water and human kindness. Whether from pity or compassion, he seemed determined to make me remember I still deserved a shred of dignity.

I had little to offer him in return. I didn't identify as gay or bi at that point, so anything sexual felt impossible unless I was too intoxicated to remember. Yet Eugene never blocked the door if I wanted to leave for another hit after three or four days. Equally important, he never shut me out when I crawled back, whimpering like a stray dog seeking shelter from the storm. Day after day, he allowed me in. And if that's not a form of love, I don't know what is. But I never learned how to love him back.

Eventually, Eugene flew home to California, and although he didn't blame me for anything, I felt I'd lost the one real kindness I'd had in years. When he left, I realized how many yesterdays I'd burned through, how far I was from anything resembling tomorrow.

The Utility Closet

With Eugene gone, I was on my own. My entire identity was that of a withering, drug-addicted, alcoholic prostitute who hustled by any means necessary—legal or otherwise. My downward spiral was so visible I barely remembered the Ivy League graduate I once was.

Each day on those streets of Reno, it felt like I was living out some slow, agonizing death sentence: the thousand-cut torture—every fresh cut bled me a little more, draining not just my blood but my hope. I had lost so much dignity that I couldn't even look at myself in reflective glass without recoiling.

With nowhere else to go, I snuck into the utility closet of Eugene's old motel. Cockroaches were my only roommates. I existed among mop buckets and rags, a literal shell of the man I'd been. When the landlord finally discovered me and threw me out, that felt like cut number 998. I thought, "This is it. I'm done." My phone call to my mother was a last-ditch gamble, convinced she'd berate me. But instead of condemnation, she offered me a lifeline. That was the moment I realized I'd hit 999 out of a thousand cuts. One more strike could finish me off, but her compassion might just save me.

Days later, I tried to sell only the second piece of crack I'd ever held and not smoked. In a moment of cosmic irony, that single sale led to the Reno Police S.E.T. team swarming me. I was arrested for Selling a Controlled Substance—and it became my rescue. As the cuffs clicked around my wrists, I finally gave up trying to outsmart the world and decided to trust something bigger than me.

Confrontation With the Courts

It was September 22, 2004, when I walked back into Parr Boulevard jail to detox. The officers knew I had intel on the smaller drug rings in Reno. They dangled a proposal: cooperate, become an informant, and drastically reduce my time. In simpler terms, snitch. If I handed them enough names, they'd let me trade prison for drug court and supervised treatment.

Snitching, in prison culture, was about the lowest thing

you could do. Especially for Black inmates, revealing inside information meant risking immediate death or a crippling beatdown. I'd seen men "roll up" into protective custody yards just to stay alive. On a previous bid, I watched a white inmate get approached by Aryan types who told him, "We know you snitched. Either you move to PC, or you don't live." He vanished to solitary the next day, while his own son, also incarcerated, disowned him.

But I was no gangster or shot-caller; I was an addict. My only loyalty was to whatever substance dulled the pain. Under the harsh glare of interrogation lights, I sang like Pavarotti. Selectively, though—feeding them outdated intel, nothing that'd get me killed. After a while, the detectives weren't satisfied. They wanted me to wear a wire, go back into the streets. That was a no-go. I knew I'd either end up dead on the street or using again. So I refused.

Staring Down the Gavel

With no wiretap assistance from me, I faced Judge James W. Hardesty once more. He leaned forward, looked me squarely in the eye, and said in a stern, disappointed tone:

"Mr. Miller, if you come into my courtroom one more time —for any felony—I will apply the habitual criminal statute. What a waste you are. You've been blessed with opportunity. You're an Ivy League graduate from a decent family. You have no excuse. Come here again, and I'll give you the full Habitual."

In Nevada, "Big Bitch" and "Little Bitch" were the dreaded

titles for habitual-offender statutes—harsh mandatory minimums running from five years to life, or even 25 to life. Judge Hardesty was basically telling me: next slip, next felony, and you're locked away for good. He rattled off my countless arrests and convictions, each one an added nail in my coffin of shame.

With a heavy sigh, he handed me six years—72 months in the state prison—for a $10 rock sale. I was stunned. The scale of it felt impossible. But in hindsight, it was probably the break I needed.

Another Journey Behind Bars

My case in Superior Court took about three months before I was shipped off to prison for the third time. Detoxed and lying on my bunk in county, I took stock of my entire life: the 13 failed inpatient treatment attempts, the bleakness of hustling on the streets, and the fact I was probably going to die if something didn't change. How did I end up here, yet again?

I'd had so much going for me once—a mother who loved me unconditionally, a decent upbringing, college opportunities, even glimpses of success in the corporate and modeling worlds. Yet I had systematically torn all that down with addiction and crime. Staring at the cold cell ceiling, I asked God, *Why can't I just quit messing up?*

That's when a quiet answer filled me—like a voice in my head that wasn't mine, telling me He was with me, always. If I let Him protect me this time, I could stay clean. Maybe it was just me talking to myself, or maybe it was a genuine spiritual moment. Either way, I believed it.

Another Chance at WINGS

Once I transferred to Northern Nevada Correctional Center, I found out I'd be placed in the WINGS Program again—a segregated unit for drug treatment. I'd done nine months in WINGS during a previous bid but never took it seriously. This time, I walked in determined to treat it like my last chance.

The environment was calmer—mostly older inmates, men who'd been battered by life and recognized the value of real recovery. We had separate counselors, a dedicated yard, weight-lifting equipment, and a dining hall. I was able to move around easily because I wasn't branded by any specific gang or politics. Local, helpful, not into prison politics—that was me. When others recognized my willingness to teach or help, I became a kind of tutor and friend, which also earned me a measure of respect.

Lacking money or outside support, I had no radio or TV. I filled those silent hours with books—reading 10 to 15 every month. I devoured history, biographies, self-improvement, law references—anything to keep my mind engaged. It felt like an internal transformation: I could see hope in studying, in exploring, in honest self-reflection instead of endless self-pity.

Embracing the Program

Something was different this time. It was as if my mind snapped open, allowing me to see a path forward. WINGS forced me to face my victim mentality and the fallout of blaming everything on others. I wasn't a victim. Yes, life had thrown me curveballs, but I alone had chosen to respond with lies, crimes, and addiction.

Seeing me grow in maturity, the counselors made me a mentor. I took it seriously, guiding newer arrivals through the same steps I'd once scorned. Each time I helped another man, my self-worth inched up. I recalled Gandhi's words, "Find yourself by losing yourself in service to others," and realized they rang true for me. I rediscovered a version of myself I'd lost in the madness of the streets—someone who could help, not just harm.

Among the men who visited was Augie, a white civilian volunteer who ran anonymous recovery meetings. He gave me extra reading material and the unwavering affirmation that no life is too far gone. Even in prison, gratitude settled in my chest. *I'm still alive. I still have another shot.*

One day, another inmate arrived—an older, highly educated white guy with a tragic but captivating story. Decades earlier, he'd been part of a radical group that robbed a bank in Connecticut. A cop got killed in the shootout. He went underground, found God, rebuilt his life under a new identity for 30 years—marriage, kids, a normal neighborly existence—until a simple fender-bender triggered a fingerprint check and exposed him. Now he was serving Life

Without Parole. He couldn't be in a Connecticut prison because guards might "accidentally" let him get killed for the fallen cop. Hearing his life saga taught me how a person could completely reinvent themselves. And if a man like that could find faith and acceptance within these walls, maybe so could I.

Dumped, Then Determined

After a full year in WINGS, they transferred me back to general population. I carried over my journaling, tutoring, and quiet devotion. About four months later—month 16—I finally got a parole hearing. It was denied. *Dumped,* as we say inside. I crumbled at first, desperate to leave. But lying on my bunk, I prayed for understanding. It dawned on me: I wasn't ready. I'd done programs before and relapsed, repeating my cycle. Another year inside might be exactly what I needed to cement my foundation.

They assigned me to teach English as a Second Language (ESL) to Hispanic inmates, even though I barely spoke a word of Spanish. We muddled through. I also stumbled onto two hustles: (1) being the prison photographer, unofficially snapping Polaroids for those wanting to show their tattoos, their groups, or even risqué pictures for pen-pal "boyfriends"; (2) writing letters for illiterate or older convicts. Payment was always stamps, which were currency on the yard.

Taking pictures was delicate. We were basically running contraband images, risky enough that the warden could've hauled me off to solitary if caught. In a place where people angle for blackmail, I had to maintain ironclad confidentiality. A single slip could spark trouble for me or them. But it paid in stamps—a lifeline for correspondence, trades, or even occasional extra food.

Ghostwriting letters was equally tricky. Old-timers needed help writing to families, pastors, or lawyers. I'd glean personal histories some men never revealed out loud. Trust was paramount. I had to capture their raw emotions in words that remained private. A single misspoken line in a letter could fan the flames of family drama or prison politics. Once, my bunkie asked me to pen a letter to his girlfriend. Tired from a long day, I told him I'd do it tomorrow. Mistake. He blocked the window in our cell and started wrapping his hands, preparing for a fight. In his eyes, my refusal to write it immediately was disrespect. I defused the situation eventually, but it was a sobering reminder: prison has its own rhythms of respect and swift retaliation.

Through it all, I kept my head down, leaning on my newfound faith and self-worth. I stuck to tutoring, reading, and avoiding any scenario that might threaten my promise to myself: no more wasted chances. Then, at the next parole hearing—28 months total into this sentence—they granted me release. I'd entered NNCC as a hollowed-out husk, nearing death. Now, I was stepping out with real hope.

A Final Day Behind Bars

Packing my small allotment of property that final day, I felt a trembling rush. Could this be the last time I ever walked these corridors? Handing in my uniforms, returning my bunk's flattened pillow, I realized I was no longer the dope-fueled creature who first arrived. This time, I was clearer, more centered, and wholeheartedly committed to sobriety.

After the final ride in the prison van, I stepped into a nearby casino for a meal. The staff handed me "drink tokes" after I paid the check—a courtesy or enticement. Looking at them, I almost laughed. These were the same tokens I used to pocket and trade for free booze—the same freebies that once guaranteed I'd stay trapped in my old habits. Now I handed them back and shook my head. *No, I'm good.* It was a small moment, but it felt monumental. I drank some water, savoring the simple ability to choose self-preservation over self-destruction.

I walked out of that casino into the sun, carrying more than just a prison release slip—I carried a fragile optimism that maybe, this time, I'd do things differently.

CHAPTER 12: MY REFLECTIONS

The biggest fight often starts after you walk out those gates. The old temptations lurk, the same triggers wait in the free world. But if you've built a sturdy foundation—both spiritual and practical—you stand a better chance at enduring. And once you say no to the drink tokes, you're actively rewriting your next chapter.

1. **No Act of Kindness Is Wasted** - Eugene wasn't just a fleeting shelter. He was proof that compassion survives in the harshest realities. Even if you're not ready to accept it fully, a spark of kindness can remind you that you're not beyond redemption.
2. **Bargaining with the System** - Snitching or "*selective confession*" can feel like an easy out, but it also drags you into a labyrinth of prison politics. When your only loyalty is to your next high, you're prone to dangerous choices. Facing that reality without a wire or new hustles means confronting who you really are.
3. **Consequences Are Real** - Seventy-two months for a $10 rock sale sounds outrageous—until you consider the consistent chain of crimes behind it. By the time you're labeled a repeat offender, judges

and statutes clamp down hard. "*Big Bitch*" or "*Little Bitch*," the system doesn't care about your backstory once you cross that line again.

4. **Second Chances Need Work** - Programs like WINGS can be a joke if you're not ready. The difference lies in willingness—pushing aside self-pity and embracing the idea that you alone own your recovery. No counselor or sponsor can force it on you.
5. **Trust Earns Respect, and Vice Versa** - Inside prison, small reputations grow quickly—helping people, teaching, or just keeping your word can earn you space to breathe. But one betrayal or slip can close doors fast. That principle applies outside as well. When you show up consistently, people notice.

PART FIVE

REDEMPTION, RECONNECTION, & REINVENTION

CHAPTER 13
RELEASE & REBUILDING

I was ecstatic to be free again. Matthew flew in from L.A. to pick me up. Throughout my bid, we'd kept in contact, and he'd fallen deeply in love with me—or at least with the idea of me. He was convinced we'd built a foundation for a great relationship, and he felt sure I was just as invested. I was excited too—but only as a friend. I'd never envisioned partnering romantically with another man, though I'd welcomed his company during some of my loneliest times on the inside.

I was released in Carson City, Nevada, and asked Matthew to drive me back to Reno. Feeling that warm desert air against my face was almost surreal. My mind raced with what-ifs—possibilities for sobriety and a fresh start, but also guilt over how I'd led Matthew on. No part of me intended to continue a relationship with someone who also fought his own battles with sobriety. We both knew what relapse felt like, and romantic entanglements with someone so new to recovery felt like lighting a match in a room full of gas fumes.

Guilt on the Road Back

During the drive, memories of Matthew and me rolled through my thoughts: the laughter in treatment, the nights waiting for test results, the heartbreak of watching friends die of AIDS. But there was another realization. On the streets, my eyes had always been fixed below eye level. That's where people dropped rocks of crack, money, and tokens—where danger flared. I'd never looked up. Now, for the first time, I consciously lifted my gaze. I noticed the sky stretching over desert mountains, so open and endless that it felt like freedom itself.

Guilt hit me, too. I'd been using Matthew, maybe not maliciously, but enough to recognize I wasn't being a true friend. A part of me wanted to keep his support, but another part knew I had to be honest—for both our sakes. Looking up at that wide sky, I understood my world was bigger than it had ever been on the streets. And I realized I still had so much work to do on myself.

We arrived in Reno, and Matthew booked a room. When he stepped out, I found myself in that critical 24–48-hour period after release—when every choice can steer you toward freedom or right back to a cell. My dream was to look in the mirror and genuinely like who I saw. To achieve that, I needed an environment that supported sobriety, not a half-measure where I'd be stuck in an emotional tug-of-war.

So I left. I walked out before he came back. I chose to look up and walk away. He never forgave me for that. And I had to accept it.

Walking across Reno wasn't easy. Old temptations crowded every street corner. Minute by minute, I fought the urge to swing by familiar spots. It took me nearly four hours of pushing past each craving to reach a halfway house on the corner of 2nd and Keystone. That was my first step in consciously controlling my surroundings—removing excuses to use.

The Reality of The Road Ahead

Once I settled in, I confronted how quickly small missteps could become giant pitfalls. One night, I got into a heated argument with the house manager for violating curfew. No illicit activity on my part—I just miscalculated travel time. But I recognized how a single "acceptable" excuse could put me back in the mindset of, "Well, I messed up anyway, might as well use." Even the simplest human error could become my reason to relapse.

I realized something about myself: I had always been an addict looking for an excuse. My best defense was strict order —a conscious effort to keep my life structured so chaos wouldn't overtake me. For years, I'd hustled people and manipulated circumstances. Now, I was hustling myself toward a new life. But order comes with a side effect: boredom. When everything is organized and predictable, I start to itch for something to stir up the routine. Sometimes I wondered if that's why God, as the story goes, let the universe explode into existence: to have something new to create and fix. Either way, I pushed forward. Boredom was a small price to pay for staying clean.

That same day I arrived in Reno, I contacted my first sponsor, Augie. He used to bring meetings into the prison, so I trusted him. We grabbed dinner, and I eagerly ordered a double bacon cheeseburger. After so long without pork, that salty taste felt like heaven. Augie, clean for over 25 years, asked if I was ready to truly work a program or keep letting my "old programming" run me. I vowed I was all in, hungry for genuine change.

After dinner, he dropped me off at the halfway house and offered to sponsor me. I immediately agreed—until he gave his first directive: "No relationships for a year." I stammered, complaining that I'd had no real relationship for three years already. But he insisted. And deep down, I knew why. If I couldn't keep myself stable, there was no sense dragging someone else into my chaos. Sobriety had to come first, no matter how lonely or difficult.

A New Mindset

Over the next few days, I thought back to a revelation I'd had in prison, lying on my bunk and asking, "How did I get here?" The answer stung: my own thinking and my own choices had funneled me into addiction, homelessness, and criminal records—costing me years of my life. I realized the same mind that got me there wouldn't get me out. Einstein said it best: "The thinking that got you into the problem won't get you out of it."

I also saw that I'd never really demonstrated adult sobriety before. My longest dry spell dated back to the early '90s, and I'd relapsed as soon as an emotional trigger appeared. This time, I needed maturity—the ability to recognize my excuses and reject them before they pulled me under. So, I leaned into my new programming. I tracked everything—my diet, my exercise, my sleep. Denying myself instant gratification became the antidote to a lifetime of chasing quick highs.

Augie also reminded me that "you are who you hang out with," so I clung to safe spaces and supportive people. I avoided old dealers, friends who were still using, and any place that smelled like a party. In this delicate phase, I was protecting myself from the one excuse I knew could send me spiraling.

Of course, I questioned whether Augie's rule—no relationships for a year—was too harsh. But my track record proved my decisions were downright destructive. Augie had 25 years of continuous sobriety and had helped countless men stay clean. If I was serious about living, not just surviving, I had to trust the wisdom of someone who'd fought the same battles and won.

So I did. And the strangest thing happened. By following this guided path—by truly surrendering to the process—I started to believe I could stay sober for good. For the first time in my life, I saw discipline as strength, not punishment. I could look up, look forward, and not be terrified by what came next. Yes, I was still the same man who'd made countless mistakes. But I was also learning to be someone new—

someone who, with the right structure and mindset, could finally handle freedom on the outside.

Renegotiating the Boundaries

By the time I'd settled into life on the outside, I was in excellent shape. People noticed me wherever I went, including at recovery meetings. Women openly propositioned me for sex, and I have to admit, if I'd looked unsightly or lacked social skills, it might've made things simpler. But I was a decent-looking, charismatic guy who could hold a conversation—qualities that had led me into trouble more than once.

I approached my sponsor, Augie, with a dilemma: it had been three years since I'd had sex, and now I was struggling with intense urges. Rationally, I couldn't find any direct link between sex itself and addiction. So I tried to renegotiate the "no relationships" rule with Augie. He reminded me that early recovery should be defined alongside a trusted advisor or professional, so he appreciated me being open about it. Maturity, he said, was what most of his sponsees lacked—trying to heal from a chaotic love life in the first stages of sobriety rarely ended well.

Augie advised me to keep my focus on building consistent habits that supported my growth. I needed to become stronger in my recovery than I was in chasing my next fix. If I was going to search for an excuse, he wanted me to look for an excuse to stay sober rather than one that might pull me back into addiction.

Landmines and Environment Control

Sobriety, Augie explained, is a habit—one that must become more powerful than my compulsions or desires. Controlling my environment was crucial. As he put it, relationships early in recovery are riddled with emotional landmines: unexpected triggers that can blow up your progress without warning.

My past was littered with such landmines—impulsive hookups, unwanted pregnancies, and heartbreaks that sent me reeling. Whenever someone left me, disappointed me, or refused to give me what I wanted, I'd find a reason to use. I had zero ability to sweep for hidden bombs in the emotional minefield. Augie's point was simple: if you don't put yourself in harm's way, you don't get blown up. So I cut out every possible trigger—no substances in the house, no crack pipes, no casual beers. I went to meetings regularly, restricted my relationships, and leaned on trusted advisors.

I'd always wrestled with the idea of a "higher power." But every time I did things my way—relying on intellect or hustle alone—I ended up on the brink of death. Being accountable to a higher source, no matter what I called it, was one of the keys to staying clean.

Eventually, Augie said I could have sex—just no serious relationships. That was the new ground rule. Naturally, the moment I got that green light, I couldn't seem to find a single healthy prospect. It was like some cosmic joke: when I was off-limits, I had lines out the door; now that I'd gotten permission, I couldn't pick up a woman if I was King Kong.

Despite that, I continued sharing my story at meetings, trying to help newcomers. On Tuesdays, I visited different groups to speak, and on Saturdays, I took men along to meetings. After one talk, a woman asked if I could drive her to another meeting. The chemistry between us was electric. She made it clear I could have her anytime I wanted—but she'd only been sober a week. I told her we could talk after she'd hit 30 days.

When she reached that milestone, she was granted an overnight pass. I picked her up in my sharp '95 Buick Riviera with gold trim, thinking I'd finally see some action. But God had other plans: I got slammed with horrible food poisoning that night. We ended up doing nothing, and I was forced to confront how close I'd come to stepping over a line I wasn't ready to cross. I realized I still had work to do on myself.

An Emotional Trigger Event

A few weeks later, on a warm July night, I offered to pick up another woman, Carrie, for a meeting. She was early in her recovery too, but when I arrived, I found her drunk. Everything in me screamed to turn around and leave her there. Instead, I accepted her advances and slept with her.

I drove away afterward feeling ashamed. I had been in a position of authority, and I should've protected both her and myself. I knew we couldn't keep seeing each other if she was actively using. The risk of relapse was just too high. I vowed then and there never to do it again.

But late that summer, my phone rang: it was Carrie. She

told me she was pregnant—and I was the father. It turned out later that she was not pregnant, but I did not know that at the time.

My heart plummeted. In that moment, I knew I had messed up in more ways than I could count. Carrie's call triggered the most intense cravings I'd had in years. I was right on the edge of using, desperate to block out the panic. Then a thought—like a switch—cut through the chaos: Who's really the director of my life?

I realized only two entities truly understand why a person does something: the person themselves and God. If I insisted on directing my own life without a spiritual connection, I'd keep careening off the rails. I'd proven that more than once. Now, it felt like God was challenging me to confront this test—a point of friction that demanded either real change or the same old destructive patterns.

I knew one thing: I wouldn't wish my addiction on my worst enemy, let alone my unborn child. I chose sobriety.

Turning Inward and Moving Forward

Back in prison, I'd started working on five key areas of my well-being: physical, intellectual, spiritual, emotional, and my addiction itself. Whenever life threw me off balance, I returned to those fundamentals. I realized no external fix—no fancy program, no perfect sponsor—could force me to stay clean if I wasn't willing to do the inner work.

The first step was surrender. I stopped fighting God and accepted that a higher principle or power was guiding me toward better decisions. For too long, I'd let fear and pleasure dictate my choices. I saw time as a loan from God; every experience either added value or subtracted from it. Facing this unplanned pregnancy showed me I needed to see the gift in my pain. Pain reminded me I was still alive, still capable of growth, still able to ask for help before it was too late.

I shifted to address my intellect next. I knew I had to reframe the way I thought about my past and my worth. Yes, I was academically gifted. I could speak in a formal setting about "parsimonious men" or rephrase it in the starkest street language. But none of that made me a genius at living life. I'd learned not to judge or look down on people who had less formal education. We were all just humans—often with secrets we hid behind closed doors.

Secrets, I came to see, can strangle self-esteem. They're like prisoners in the back of your mind, but in truth, they hold you hostage. You convince yourself that if anyone knew your real truth—your darkest mistakes—they'd never love you. That fear makes you keep lying, keep hiding, keep hustling.

I started asking bigger questions: Am I lovable? What if everyone sees the real me? That terror of rejection had fueled so many of my worst decisions. Even as a grown man, I needed the acceptance of others to validate my worth. If a psychiatrist once called my ethics "situational," I finally understood why: I was willing to shift my morals, break promises, and even break my own heart just to feel included.

I realized I wasn't alone. Christians with secret transgressions, social media users desperate for likes, men with multiple partners who each validate a different aspect of their fragile egos—we all had the same fundamental issue: an inability to love ourselves without external props.

Stepping back, I saw how far I'd come—yet how much remained. My emotional triggers, my secrets, and my addiction had all collided with the news of Carrie's pregnancy, forcing me to confront another crossroads. But for once, I didn't run to the nearest fix. I didn't drown in guilt or shame. I held onto my newfound conviction that, if I surrendered to a higher power and kept control of my environment, I could keep building a life I wouldn't be ashamed of.

CHAPTER 13: MY REFLECTIONS

Stepping out of prison walls did not guarantee genuine freedom. I had to learn to navigate the landmines of early recovery—old relationships, new temptations, and the unsettling truth that no environment is entirely safe unless I'm willing to protect it. In confronting these truths, I've found that freedom isn't a one-time event; it's a steady process of staying mindful, staying open, and staying committed—even when every emotion screams for the quick fix. With each test, I learn a little more about the man I'm becoming and the life I'm striving to build.

1. **Emotional Landmines Are Everywhere** - What seems harmless—like meeting someone at a recovery group or rekindling a friendship—can suddenly detonate if you're not cautious. Early sobriety is especially volatile; staying vigilant about potential triggers or unstable partners can keep one bad decision from unraveling your progress.
2. **Secrets Keep You Hostage** - Locking away your past—whether it's sexual escapades, hustles, or deep emotional wounds—doesn't bury the pain; it buries *you*. A secret is more like a prison guard

than a prisoner. The fear that "*no one will accept me if they know everything*" often drives us to repeat the same mistakes. Real freedom begins when you're honest with yourself and those you trust.

3. **One Excuse Can Undo It All** - Recovery requires constant commitment to environment, mindset, and spiritual grounding. All it takes is a single "*perfectly understandable*" excuse—a rough day, a moment of shame, or even a burst of pride—to topple the whole structure. A key tactic is replacing old justifications to use with new justifications to stay sober.
4. **Uncomfortable Accountability Pays Off** - Saying "no" to Matthew, turning down casual sex with someone freshly sober, or walking away from a tempting environment can feel cruel or lonely in the moment. But these choices protect long-term sobriety. True accountability may sting, but it shields you from deeper regrets that can haunt you for years.
5. **Surrender Is Strength** - Time and again, trying to run the show alone led to destructive outcomes. Recognizing a higher power—God, a guiding principle, or anything bigger than your ego—can anchor you. When life throws an unexpected twist, that spiritual connection provides the clarity to choose your best path rather than your most familiar one.

6. **Pain as a Prompt for Growth** - Feeling guilt or shame instead of numbing it is a sign of healing. Pain is often a warning signal from your conscience or a nudge from something greater. If you can face it—rather than flee—you'll find it lessens its power over you and opens the door to lasting change.

CHAPTER 14
GRACE FROM ABOVE & WITHIN

Addressing secrets and building self-esteem requires grounding in truth. It often means looking backward to trace the source of our behaviors—which in turn demands we identify what we're really wrestling with. Once we pinpoint the issue, there are only three conversations we can have.

The first conversation is with a higher power. Some call it God, Spirit, Source, Allah, Yahweh—or some other name for an entity that can alter our behavior or shift our hearts. We access this presence through prayer, meditation, or deeply focused reflection.

The second conversation is with external sources. This is the most common—and least reliable—level of communication. It's filtered through the other person's perception and vocabulary, and further distorted by our own internal filters. Ask twenty people you respect to define the color burgundy, and you might get fifteen or twenty versions. It's the same with any conversation we have with others. Testimony can be flawed, so the truth we receive is always a blend of multiple lenses.

Finally, we can have a conversation with ourselves. This, I believe, is the most crucial. Our self-talk is constant, instant, and shapes every experience we have—even our perceptions of what we hear from God. No human being is exempt from this. So, if we truly want to change our self-worth, we have to learn to manage that internal dialogue and extend grace to ourselves.

The Transformative Power Of Grace

Grace, as I see it, involves allowance, forgiveness, or space. It's not weakness; in fact, it's a sign of profound maturity. When I talk about allowance, I mean recognizing that we're human beings—not just human doings. Our journey of becoming is formed in that acceptance. Even in monetary terms, an "allowance" is a sign of appreciation that you've grown enough to contribute. For me, grace also includes forgiveness: a voluntary choice to release someone from the need for retaliation or payback, even when they hurt you. That doesn't mean ignoring consequences; it means you're not carrying a vendetta in your heart. Finally, space is the gap between an event and our reaction—a critical moment when we can step away from instinctive retaliation and choose a different path.

Apologies vs. Amends

- **Apology**: A verbal or emotional admission of regret. I've told my mother "I'm sorry" countless times after relapsing. I meant it. But apologies alone rarely heal the deepest wounds.
- **Amends**: Acknowledging you caused harm, accepting the suffering you created, expressing genuine remorse, changing your behavior, and attempting to repair damage if possible. For instance, the young lady I never escorted to her abortion deserved far more than just "I'm sorry." I'd caused emotional trauma through my reckless decisions and abandonment. She may never fully recover, but by making amends, I let her know I realize the depth of my wrongs—and that I'm striving to live differently now.

When combined, a sincere apology plus true amends brings real peace of mind. It reassures the hurt party that their pain is validated and regretted. At the same time, making amends helps you stop hating yourself for what you did. You can rest easier, knowing you tried to right the wrong.

Sometimes, we can't get clean or stay sober because we've done things that make us despise ourselves. We might apologize, but if there's a lurking fear we'll do it again, or if we can't accept our own humanity, we stay stuck. Self-forgiveness becomes the hardest task. I've realized it's often simpler to forgive someone else than to release resentment toward our own reflection—because memory stores the emotions and replays them whenever we recall the hurt. In that sense, we create our own private hell, burning ourselves alive with unforgiveness.

Grace In Action

Space is that brief span between an event and the action we take. One day, I was limping around a Reno motel after my jaw had been broken for the second time. I came face-to-face with the man who did it. A 32-ounce beer bottle in my hand, I was seconds from bashing him for revenge. But in that gap—in that fraction of a moment—I hesitated. He begged for mercy, claimed he was high and out of his mind. I granted him the space to walk past. I granted that space to myself, too.

Had I swung that bottle, I could've killed or paralyzed him—and ended up in prison for years. Instead, we both lived our separate lives. That gap is where thousands of people get trapped in regret, perpetually wishing they'd chosen a different door. But when we allow ourselves a moment to think—without immediate reaction—we give grace not only to the other person but also to our future selves.

It's much simpler to end something than to nurture it. Ending a relationship after infidelity is straightforward; giving it another chance with real allowance and forgiveness is much tougher.

Grace Toward Ourselves

I discovered that offering grace to others helped me connect more deeply with a version of myself I actually liked. Rather than defining myself by every mistake, I learned to say, "I've done terrible things" instead of "I am a terrible person." One is rooted in guilt—the other in shame. Guilt acknowledges a regrettable action; shame insists you're destined to remain that way.

I recognized how many times I'd been extended grace by others—my mom, judges, friends I ripped off, women I hurt. Once, in a grimy motel room, I was going at a guy we called "Sheik," mocking him relentlessly. High and drunk, I ignored his warnings. Suddenly, he had a knife pressed to my chest. If he'd pushed it deeper, I was dead. There was no doubt in my mind. I saw his tears—he didn't want to kill me, but I'd insulted and disrespected him in front of everyone. He had his own script of pride that demanded a show of force.

Faced with death, I begged for mercy. And he gave it. He extended grace, standing in the gap long enough to let me live. That moment hammered home the reality: grace can flip the script. It can spare both parties from a life of regret.

Desire To Become More

I used to wrap my identity in all the things I'd done—like wearing layers of embroidered jackets. Each one bore a name or a memory: pimp, hustler, addict, inmate, dropout. Many of those experiences put me inches from death—my own or someone else's. I felt ashamed and unable to love myself. The real shift came when I learned to extend grace to myself. I began applauding my strengths and working on my weaknesses, giving both room to breathe. I accepted that I'd still make mistakes on this journey of becoming, but those mistakes would just be things I'd done—not the sum of who I was.

I came to see who I am as the vision in my head of the man I will be when I take my final breath. Every moment before that is just part of the transformation. In a way, I forgave myself in advance for future missteps, trusting they'd be lessons I hadn't yet learned. After all, it takes 98 years to become a 98-year-old. I no longer wanted to simply exist; I wanted to do life well.

Rebuilding Body and Mind

Physically, I was in good shape—thanks to healthy habits I picked up behind bars, like weightlifting and boxing. I joined a local basketball league in Reno, and I poured my energy into working on myself—whether in the gym or in regular life. My mother's health was failing from congestive heart failure, and I wanted to cherish every minute with her. I'd already learned the hard way what it felt like to lose a parent before showing them the sober adult you could become.

About that time, I met a beautiful woman who invited me to go running. Running wasn't my thing, but I went anyway. Our first outing was a slow jog, and I spent most of it trailing her—though I didn't mind because I had a perfect view. The first fifteen minutes burned like hell, but once my body realized I wasn't quitting, it went numb and let me push forward. Sometimes it felt like I could run forever with her in front. I'd play mind games to distract myself from pain—imagining I was running for my mom, or for some important cause, or maybe just to catch up with my running partner. Over time, I started doing 5Ks and 10Ks until running became a passion. I replaced thoughts of pain with new motivations, and soon I was clocking more than ten miles a session, feeling free every time I laced up my shoes.

Revisiting Dartmouth—and Other Doors

My life improved, and I realized it was time to walk through more "doors" of unresolved issues. I'd been journaling, cataloging every piece of unfinished business that still caused me anxiety or regret. I started with Dartmouth, that old wound in my past. For years, I'd claimed to be a Dartmouth grad, but technically I still owed them a class—and possibly some money. Fear (or "False Evidence Appearing Real") kept me from reaching out. In my head, they'd never forgive me or let me back in.

When I finally mustered the courage to contact them, I discovered the school had written off the debt decades ago. They didn't want my money—they just wanted me to finish that one outstanding course. So I enrolled at the University of Alaska as a forty-something man surrounded by fresh-faced kids, struggling through material I hadn't touched in years. But I pushed on and earned that last credit. My Dartmouth diploma arrived in the mail soon after. The next thing I knew, I was starting an alumni chapter in Anchorage, attending reunions, sitting on committees, and mentoring current students—enthusiastic about helping them avoid the minefields I once stepped in. I went from dreading Dartmouth to embracing it and making a real impact. It reminded me how fear had blocked me from a freedom that was mine all along.

Making Amends Where Possible

Next came my first wife, Chrissy. We'd married for convenience more than love, and then I walked out on her without warning—an incredibly selfish act. I was terrified to reach out, expecting she'd scream at me or never speak to me again. But again, I stepped through that imaginary door. I called, and she actually answered. It turned out she'd done her own healing; she forgave me. All those nightmare scenarios I'd played in my head were just False Evidence Appearing Real once again.

I started reaching out to anyone I recalled hurting. Every addict leaves victims in their wake, whether they intend to or not. One person I desperately tried to find was Siri, a teenage girl who'd been a working girl for years before I met her. I used to pimp her, even though she genuinely loved me. I betrayed that love by leaving her alone with three thugs who treated her like an object. It haunts me how I saw the disappointment in her eyes that day. I've searched for her every year since I got out—in missions, jails, hometown records—and come up empty. If Siri ever reads these words, I want her to know: I'm deeply, profoundly sorry. If I could rewind time, I'd take away that betrayal and never abandon her trust. I pray life has treated her better than I did.

Not every open door was about me causing harm. Sometimes it was about loss: I never had a choice in losing my brother, Jacob. As kids in foster care, we were separated when I got adopted. I've spent years trying to track him down. I'm willing to fly anywhere, talk to anyone, if it means finding him again. But so far, every trail has gone cold. He's still my brother, my twin at heart, and always will be—even if we never meet again this side of eternity. I carry him in my soul wherever I go.

Establishing a New Life

Meanwhile, I kept strengthening my spiritual, intellectual, emotional, and physical health. Upon returning to Anchorage, I dedicated myself to building a stable life. I owed about $2,800 to various people, plus $8,000 to the IRS. Determined to settle my debts, I used the "snowball method," tackling them one by one. In Reno, I'd started at a warehouse job for six bucks an hour, capped at 32 hours a week. Even so, I lived responsibly—eventually earning enough to get my own apartment, a milestone I'd never reached before. A few promotions later, I was making $11 an hour, better than anything in my past. The new Ken took pride in paying debts, not avoiding them. Each bill I cleared felt like another door opening, another weight off my shoulders.

I came to realize that whether it was physically running

ten miles or knocking on an old emotional door, pain and fear couldn't hold me forever if I refused to quit. The more I faced what I'd avoided—debts, regrets, broken connections—the more I discovered that my biggest enemy was never someone else's judgment. It was the lie that I wasn't worthy of healing, of success, of closure. One by one, I'm learning to silence that voice and step boldly into every room that once had me trembling outside the door.

CHAPTER 14: MY REFLECTIONS

Each "*unfinished door*" we choose to open brings us closer to who we're meant to be. We learn that often the biggest barrier is our own self-doubt. And once we dare to push past it, we discover possibilities that free us from shame, fear, and regret —and move us further along the path of genuine, lasting transformation.

1. **Self-Identity Isn't Locked in Your Past** - You're not forever tied to the worst things you've done. Instead of "*I am a failure,*" say "*I've done failing things.*" That shift turns shame into guilt you can address—and ultimately redeem.
2. **Face the Fear (False Evidence Appearing Real)** - So many times, I built up nightmares of how people would react if I reached out. Reality was often much kinder than my imagination. Pushing through that fear opens doors you thought were locked.
3. **Physical Challenges Can Mirror Spiritual Ones** - Running became a metaphor for my life: push past the initial pain, settle into a rhythm, and find your stride. Embracing discomfort in one area can strengthen resolve across all areas.

4. **Making Amends Is About Growth, Not Guarantees** - Not everyone will accept your apology or respond with forgiveness. Some people hold onto anger; some vanish. But making amends is vital for **your** healing—whether or not they ever reciprocate.
5. **Stay Accountable, Even When It's Hard** - Whether it's paying off debt or finishing a missing course, loose ends drain your mental and emotional energy. Completing them isn't just a task—it's a statement that you're serious about becoming whole.
6. **Never Stop Searching for What Matters** - For me, that's my brother Jacob, or a girl named Siri who deserved better. Whatever (or whoever) you've lost, keep your heart open. Even if you never find them, you'll find the best in yourself along the way.

CHAPTER 15
BECOMING KEN

A year after leaving prison, I moved back to Anchorage and landed a supervisor job at the Dena'ina Convention Center. My team oversaw concessions, including alcohol sales, which meant I spent a lot of time around liquor carts—measuring bottles and consolidating inventory. Amazingly, even when alcohol spilled on my fingers, I felt no urge to taste it. It was as if the old romance with booze—that destructive lover who was thrilling yet toxic—had finally ended. In its place, I found a healthier passion. I was still hitting the gym, lifting weights, and playing basketball—pouring my energy into physical pursuits that kept my mind clear and my heart strong.

A Mentor and an Injury

One day at the gym, I struck up a conversation with a guy who looked familiar. We realized we'd previously worked together, and he introduced himself as Jim—soon becoming my first mentor in Alaska. Not long after, while playing basketball, I injured my right Achilles. Thinking it was just a sprain, I hobbled around for a few days until finally seeing a doctor. It turned out my tendon was completely torn, requiring surgery.

Before the operation, I was blunt with the medical team: "I'm an addict," I told them. I'd heard too many relapse stories about people prescribed pain meds after surgery. I refused to fall into that trap. Initially, I argued against any medications at all; eventually, we agreed on a plan. My post-op Percocet and Tylenol 3 prescriptions would go straight to my chaperone, and I'd use them minimally. After one day on Percocet, I switched to Tylenol 3, then quickly downgraded to aspirin. Throughout, I kept in close contact with my sponsor. I didn't fear relapse so much as I respected it—knowing the darkness it could bring if I lowered my guard.

Recovery took about a month. My job and I parted ways by mutual agreement, so I turned to my mentor, Mr. Posey, for guidance. He suggested I check out Bean's Café—a local soup kitchen in downtown Anchorage that was hiring for an Executive Director. Eager for a fresh opportunity, I walked in, introduced myself, and asked about the ED position. The man who greeted me—Jim Crockett—informed me with a laugh that he was the Executive Director and had no plans to vacate. But he did mention they needed a Development Director, essentially a fundraiser for the nonprofit.

On-the-Spot Confidence

With zero fundraising experience, I boldly asked to see their books and declared I could boost their revenue by $400,000 within a year. Mr. Crockett raised an eyebrow but decided to take me upstairs to meet Bernard Washington, Bean's Financial Officer. The moment Mr. Washington heard that Mr. Posey had referred me, I felt doors opening wide. It reminded me of Stephen Covey's principle from *The Speed of Trust*: the greatest opportunities in life often hinge on who you know—and who knows you. Thanks to these relationships, I got the chance to prove myself.

I refused to let these men down. I devoured books on fundraising and connected with every resource I could find, immersing myself in the local fundraising community. I joined the Association for Fundraising Professionals, worked seven days a week, and arrived early, staying late. This wasn't just a job. Having spent sixteen years in missions and soup kitchens myself, I knew how vital these places were for people on the edge. By the end of that year, my $400,000 goal seemed almost modest—I raised closer to $700,000.

Paying It Forward: Mentorship

My next priority was giving back to young men—mentoring them the way others had mentored me. At an NAACP event where I received the President's Award, I gave an off-the-cuff speech about the need for experienced Black men to guide the younger generation. That led me to my first mentee, a bright young man who went on to earn his MBA from Oxford. Mentoring became a key way I sustained my sense of purpose and value. Just like Augie's guidance had shaped me, I wanted to pass that wisdom on to others—especially those who might be wrestling with challenges I knew all too well.

Along the way, I learned that every mentor needs mentors of his own. My mother remained my number one source of inspiration, but men like Jim, Mr. Washington, and Mr. Posey brought new dimensions of guidance. They reminded me that mentorship is a two-way street—each of us has lived experiences the other can benefit from. I discovered that my years in prison, my street background, and my business savvy formed an unusual but effective toolkit for helping others. The honesty I demanded from myself in recovery translated into honest reflections for them.

Focusing on Boundaries

I was also mindful of how easy it is to cross lines in mentorship, especially if you don't define healthy boundaries. Men, and particularly young Black men, often lack safe spaces to talk about fatherhood, relationships, pride, or self-esteem. Those conversations go deep, building a bond where vulnerability thrives. I decided early on I wouldn't mentor women one-on-one—an environmental control to avoid the messy gray areas that can arise if people confuse emotional intimacy with romantic involvement. My role was to add value to a mentee's life, not create more chaos.

Part of that commitment to healthy roles meant recognizing what I gained from mentoring. It offered me a form of amends for the lost years I spent absent from my community, fueling my sense of purpose. Nothing compares to looking someone in the eye and saying, "I believe in you, and I'm proud of you," then watching them rise to meet that encouragement. Each time I help a young man glimpse his own potential, my own courage reservoir refills.

My Mother's Final Chapter

All the while, my mother's health kept declining. In 2010, she told me she didn't have long. By then, she'd moved to Lockwood, Nevada, and I found her shockingly frail at only ninety-three pounds. Her chest kept filling with fluid that needed draining—a painful procedure she grew weary of. She missed Dennis, certain she'd reunite with him in the afterlife.

I spent Saturdays at her side, determined to give her the sober son she'd always deserved. We shared deep, unhurried conversations—something I'd denied her all those years I'd been too busy getting high or locked up. We watched old Steve McQueen movies like The Blob, and if she craved pizza, I got her pizza. She'd earned the right to indulge on her own terms.

One day, she asked me to buy myself a blue blazer—one of those classic pieces she'd insisted every gentleman owns. While I was gone, she struggled in the bathroom for two hours. By the time I returned, her eyes carried a steely resolve. "Kenneth," she said softly, "I'm ready." It gutted me to hear those words, but I knew she was done fighting. This was her time, not mine.

Her close friends from the White Orchid community came over. A doctor friend had provided pills—one to help her sleep, another to slow her heart until it stopped. I crushed the first, releasing its time-release feature so it would work faster. A strange sense of relief washed over me: I'd once feared I might be capable of harming my mom for inheritance money, but now, helping her go gently revealed how untrue that was—just more "False Evidence Appearing Real" about who I thought I could become.

I told stories about our life together, tears rolling down my face. Her friends listened, comforting me. Between labored breaths, Mom managed a last bit of humor, threatening to be "mad" if her plan didn't work. Soon, her breathing slowed. November 10, 2010—the day the greatest angel I'd ever known finally took her leave.

Grieving with Love

Where I'd once been numb or apathetic in past losses, I found myself heartbroken and soul-broken at my mom's passing. If I'd ever questioned what love is, I now had my answer: love places you outside of yourself, with genuine admiration, affection, and concern for another's well-being. I didn't want my mother to leave this world, but I loved her enough to respect her choice. Gandhi's words proved true again: "Find yourself by losing yourself in service to others." Mom held on through intense pain, committed to ensuring I was okay before she left.

I had been sober for years by then, and for the first time in my life, I felt safe telling another man I loved him as a brother, as a friend, as a mentor. A year prior, knowing my mother's time was near, I'd mapped out a plan with my mentors and sponsors. When she passed, I stuck to it: I called the coroner, entrusted her body to them, then dialed my sponsor and headed straight to a meeting—despite it being the middle of the night. I also phoned other men from my network, crying and mourning openly. I realized it fulfilled them, too, to offer support in my darkest hour. Before ending my final call that night, I told my sponsor I loved him, and I knew I would be alright. It was as if Mom's final lesson had reminded me: becoming and being a source of love wasn't about controlling my life; it was about letting God work through me. When I was needed most, He provided the strength—I only had to channel it.

Founding Denali FSP, LLC

By April 2014, I was reflecting quietly on God's grace and my own path. Seven years earlier, I'd walked out of prison without ever having sent or received an email or text message. Now, I was establishing a fundraising consulting firm, Denali FSP, LLC, grateful for every twist in my story that got me here. Much of my journey has been about surviving in spite of circumstances. I've often thought I shouldn't still be standing

—shouldn't be at the level I am today. But I've watched so many, especially Black men, fail to make it out physically, emotionally, or spiritually. That's one reason I wrote this book: so others might see they can "come back" too, even if "coming back" simply means finding comfort in one's own skin and daily life.

Searching for My Birth Family

Later that same year, I decided to track down my birth parents or whatever records I could unearth. After a DNA test through Ancestry.com, I initially found few leads—just distant matches, four generations removed. Then, in November 2015, while looking up records related to Sam, I noticed a Veterans Day promotion for tracing service members through DNA. Suddenly, I got a direct hit: Donald Horne Jr., marked as my first cousin on my mother's side.

Though New York is a closed adoption state—meaning I should never have learned my birth mother's surname—I'd spent my earliest years as "Kenneth John Horne." Unbeknownst to me, that "Horne" came directly from my biological mom. I found Donald's contact info and introduced myself, explaining I was Black and biracial. He asked me to send what details I had. Once I did, he was amazed and needed to speak with his mom. I told him I was a convicted felon, an alcoholic, and a drug addict in recovery; he replied calmly, "That's not too surprising," before mentioning he'd served as an NYPD cop.

Reuniting with My Birth Mother

Over a few weeks, I honed in on two possible women who could be my mother. A friend pulled some strings via a specialized database, pinpointing Joan MacKinnon in Bloomingburg, New York—the same hometown I'd lived in with Irene until we moved to Alaska. It seemed far too coincidental. Eventually, Donald confirmed, "Yep, you're one of us!" and told me my mother was indeed Joan MacKinnon, alive and well in upstate New York. I asked him to let her know I'd be honored to talk, but would never force my way into her life if she preferred secrecy.

A few days later, he called back with her number. It was mid-December, right before a Christmas party. Though anxious, I dialed. Hearing her Irish-tinted voice for the first time, I thanked her for not aborting me. She seemed thrilled, grateful I hadn't stopped searching. We arranged to meet in February 2016. At fifty-three years old, I finally met the woman who birthed me. She was widowed, served me corned beef and cabbage, and for the first time in my life, I consciously touched my birth mother's hand—surreal beyond words.

She recognized me in old childhood pictures, recalling a day she'd seen me playing in a neighbor's yard. I discovered her brother (my uncle) had lived just a few doors from my childhood home—less than a mile from my elementary school. Growing up, we'd been practically neighbors, entirely unaware. That revelation blew my mind.

Unraveling the Story of My Father

Staying with her for a few days, I learned bits of my father's story. Mom hesitated, explaining she'd been a teenager and met another runaway girl on a bus from Boston. They ended up in a New York City rooming house, and a man there raped her. She said he went to prison. Later, my mother's sister, Aunt Cookie, added more layers: my mom had been an underage go-go dancer at the Peppermint Lounge, pregnant, and afraid to tell her parents.

She moved around, birthed me in October 1962, then moved to Queens and had my younger sister, Barbara, followed by twin boys in 1964. Those twins perished in a tragic apartment fire—one of the most haunting stories my mom shared. She even ran a bar later, courtesy of some compassionate local mafia folks, before marrying a fireman named Gordon and settling in Bloomingburg. We continued talking over the following months, until she passed away in September 2016—just seven months after I met her.

Further research revealed she was born Joanne Horne, a Canadian Irish Catholic from the Bronx. She'd run off at seventeen, ended up pregnant, and officially relinquished me to New York State by January 1963. My father was a married man named Alex Tarver, forty-two at my birth, a drug dealer and pimp from Columbus, Georgia. Legally, it was statutory rape.

My mom changed her name when she married Gordon, who'd lost a previous wife also named Joanne. I eventually found more half-siblings: older sisters—one a retired professor in Seattle, another an English teacher in upstate New York. The deeper I dug, the more I unraveled about Alex's siblings and how one uncle vanished, another was murdered, and how Alex himself died in 1978, probably from that life of hustling. I'd once daydreamed of asking him about my origins, but that hope ended with the knowledge of his death decades earlier.

Embracing My Own Imperfections

I'm now sixty-two and still wrestle with doubts—sometimes questioning my honesty, my faithfulness, my anger toward self. I catch myself in the mirror thinking, Ken, you're full of it. My wife jokes I need no external critics; I handle that job just fine. Occasionally, I'm furious about the time wasted or relationships and opportunities I ruined. But that's the universal struggle, especially among those battling addiction.

One of the harshest lies we tell ourselves is that we aren't the captains of our own ships. True, we can't control the weather or the seas—that's God or Mother Nature—but we do set the sail. That reality helped me break free from the tsunami of self-pity. Pain originates from our perceptions, not from raw events. Someone else could live my same story and use it as jet fuel to succeed. I've chosen to extend grace to the human being rather than judging the human doing. Every breath is a gift, another chance to steer a new course.

I'm grateful that most days I like who I've become. Sure,

maybe one or two percent of the time I'll dislike a bad decision I've made, but it's fleeting. I can let time and God heal me, as He always does. There's an old saying: "God may not come when you want Him, but He's always on time." If you glean nothing else from my journey, let it be this: self-initiated redemption is possible when you align yourself with God's timing. I believe in extending grace to others but also in having the courage to bestow that grace upon yourself. You are worthy of it.

A Final Word of Thanks

I began writing this book with immense apprehension, unsure how much honesty I could share. In the end, I shared everything I could, trusting that you—dear reader—might find the piece that resonates. I made sure I was emotionally safe to do so, and I hope you feel safe, too, with whatever truths you might need to face. Secrets hold no power once exposed to light, and imposters always sabotage themselves or fake success. We can do better, living in truth.

I see this entire project as me bravely revisiting each hallway of my life—foster care, Dartmouth, the streets, prison, recovery—and opening every door that didn't harm others. My prayer is that you'll do the same in your journey. This book was a dream I clutched in the darkest places, and I'm ending it brimming with gratitude for God's grace and each day I'm allowed to live. It was ultimately about surviving Ken, that lost soul I carried everywhere. But by God's grace,

I'm no longer at war with Ken. I love Ken, flaws and all. I forgive Ken. I understand Ken. I extend grace to Ken.

I am Ken Miller, and I am a kind and gentle man today.

CHAPTER 15: MY REFLECTIONS

Stepping into who we truly are often means revisiting painful chapters, confronting unexpected truths, and choosing love—even when it hurts. Whether it's losing a parent on their own terms, discovering long-lost family, or wrestling with self-doubt, each turn in the journey becomes an opportunity to realign with our deeper calling. We learn that broken pieces can be rearranged into something stronger, something meaningful—if we extend grace not just to others, but to ourselves.

1. **Love Means Letting Go** - Real love often leads us to serve another's needs above our own, even when it hurts. Sometimes it means releasing someone—like Ken did with his mom—instead of holding on out of fear. This selfless act can unlock a deeper understanding of what love truly is.
2. **Healing Isn't a Solo Act** - Asking for help and staying accountable (to sponsors, mentors, or friends) can be pivotal. Sharing our grief or fear doesn't burden others; it can also fulfill them by letting them offer genuine support. Connection is a two-way street where everyone grows.
3. **Self-Belief Outruns Circumstances** -Founding Denali FSP after prison highlights how we're more

than our past. You can learn new skills—like email or fundraising—and evolve beyond limiting beliefs. Refuse to let old labels or perceived handicaps define your potential.

4. **Curiosity Leads to Closure** - Searching for birth parents or lost relatives can open emotional floodgates. Even if the story is messy, truth-telling often dispels fears. Embracing the full picture—both uplifting and tragic—allows for genuine acceptance and healing.
5. **Extending Grace to Your Imperfections** - We all have moments of doubt, anger, or regret. Remember that pain flows from how we interpret life's events. By steering your "*ship*" wisely (even in stormy seas), you shift your perspective from helplessness to agency—and make peace with your flaws.
6. **Self-Redemption on God's Timing** - Transformation doesn't always happen when we want it, but it often arrives precisely when we're ready. Trusting that timing—even if it seems delayed—fosters patience. When you align yourself spiritually, you open the door to redemption you didn't know was possible.
7. **Honesty Defeats Impostor Syndrome** - Facing secrets and admitting hard truths strips away the power of shame. Pretending to be someone else only deepens insecurity. Authenticity is liberating for you—and a beacon of hope for others.

ACCESS THE FREE RESOURCES!

Ken Miller's Principles to Success
Pocket Guide & MORE

WWW.BECOMINGKENBOOK.COM/RESOURCES

Made in the USA
Middletown, DE
15 June 2025

77034747R00161